to

_____

from

_____

2minutes A DAY

100 DEVOTIONALS

DATING &SEX

about Godly relationships

The quoted ideas expressed in this book (but not scripture verses) are not, in all cases, exact quotations, as some have been edited for clarity and brevity. In all cases, the author has attempted to maintain the speaker's original intent. In some cases, quoted material for this book was obtained from secondary sources, primarily print media. While every effort was made to ensure the accuracy of these sources, the accuracy cannot be guaranteed. For additions, deletions, corrections or clarifications in future editions of this text, please write FAMILY CHRISTIAN PRESS.

Scripture quotations are taken from:

The Holy Bible, King James Version

The Holy Bible, New International Version (NIV) Copyright © 1973, 1978, 1984, by International Bible Society. Used by permission of Zondervan Publishing House. All rights reserved.

The New American Standard Bible®, (NASB) Copyright © 1960, 1962, 1963, 1968, 1971, 1972, 1973, 1975, 1977, 1995 by The Lockman Foundation. Used by permission.

The Holy Bible, New King James Version (NKJV) Copyright © 1982 by Thomas Nelson, Inc. Used by permission.

The Holy Bible, New Living Translation, (NLT) Copyright © 1996. Used by permission of Tyndale House Publishers, Inc., Wheaton, Illinois 60189. All rights reserved.

New Century Version®. (NCV) Copyright © 1987, 1988, 1991 by Word Publishing, a division of Thomas Nelson, Inc. All rights reserved. Used by permission.

The Holy Bible: Revised Standard Version (RSV). Copyright 1946, 1952, 1959, 1973 by the Division of Christian Education of the National Council of the Churches of Christ in the United States of America. All rights reserved. Used by permission.

The Holy Bible, The Living Bible (TLB), Copyright © 1971 owned by assignment by Illinois Regional Bank N.A. (as trustee). Used by permission of Tyndale House Publishers, Inc., Wheaton, Illinois 60189. All rights reserved.

The Message (MSG) This edition issued by contractual arrangement with NavPress, a division of The Navigators, U.S.A. Originally published by NavPress in English as THE MESSAGE: The Bible in Contemporary Language copyright 2002-2003 by Eugene Peterson. All rights reserved.

The Holman Christian Standard Bible™ (Holman CSB) Copyright © 1999, 2000, 2001 by Holman Bible Publishers. Used by permission.

Cover Design by Kim Russell / Wahoo Designs
Page Layout by Bart Dawson

ISBN 1-58334-357-1

Printed in the United States of America

100 DEVOTIONALS

DATING
&SEX

Introduction

Can you spare two minutes each day for God? Of
course you can . . . and of course you should!
Scottish-born evangelist Henry Drummond correctly
observed, "Ten minutes spent in Christ's company every
day—even two minutes—will make the whole day different."
How true. If you dedicate even a few minutes each morning
to devotional reading and prayer, you will change the tone
and direction of your life.

This book offers 100 quick devotionals about dating,
sex, and other big-time topics that are urgently important to
you, a young adult living in a temptation-filled world. On the
pages that follow, you'll find time-tested principles for taking
care of your body, your mind, your heart, and your spirit.
These lessons are intended to remind you that, if you're
wise, you'll put God in charge of every aspect of your life,
including your relationships. When you do, you'll be richly
rewarded.

So, during the next 100 days, do yourself and your world
a favor—read a chapter each day and take each day's
message to heart. Even a few short minutes, spent with God,
can change your day . . . and your life.

Day 1

Recognize the Fact that Your Choices About Dating Are Profoundly Important

The thing you should want most is God's kingdom and doing what God wants. Then all these other things you need will be given to you.

Matthew 6:33 NCV

The choices you make will determine the quality and direction of your life. And that includes all the choices you make about your dating life. As an informed citizen of the 21st century, you have every reason to make wise choices. But sometimes, when the pressures of the dating world threaten to grind you up and spit you out, you may feel tempted to make decisions that are displeasing to God. When you do, you'll suffer in more ways than you can imagine.

So, as you pause to consider the kind of Christian you are—and the kind of Christian you want to become—ask yourself whether you're sitting on the fence or standing in the light. And then, if you sincerely want to follow in the footsteps of the One from Galilee, make choices that are pleasing to Him. He deserves no less . . . and neither, for that matter, do you.

more stuff to think about

It wasn't the apple, it was the pair.

QUIPS, ANONYMOUS

To refuse to respond is in itself a response.

MADELEINE L'ENGLE

God is voting for us all the time.
The devil is voting against us all the time.
The way we vote carries the election.

CORRIE TEN BOOM

The Big Idea

Remember that the choices you make in the dating world can have a profound impact on every other aspect of your life. So, choose carefully and prayerfully.

DATING & SEX

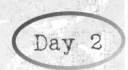
Decide Who's First
(If You Answered God,
You're Right)

You shall have no other gods before Me.
EXODUS 20:3 NKJV

Here's a quick quiz: Whose expectations are you trying to meet?
A. Your date's expectations B. Society's expectations C. God's expectations

If you're a Christian, the correct answer is C., but if you're overly concerned with either A. or B., you're not alone. Plenty of people invest too much energy trying to please their peers' (or their dates') expectations and too little energy trying to please God. It's a common behavior, but it's also a very big mistake.

A better strategy, of course, is to try to please God first. To do so, you must prioritize your life—and your relationships—according to God's commandments.

Are you having trouble choosing between God's priorities and society's priorities? Are you feeling overwhelmed or confused? If so, turn the concerns over to God—prayerfully, earnestly, and often. Then, listen for His answer . . . and trust the answer He gives.

more stuff to think about

God doesn't want shares of your life;
He wants controlling interest!

QUIPS, ANONYMOUS

When all else is gone, God is left,
and nothing changes Him.

HANNAH WHITALL SMITH

One with God is a majority.

BILLY GRAHAM

The Big Idea

Place God first in every aspect of your life, including your
dating life: He deserves first place, and any relationship that
doesn't put Him there is the wrong relationship for you.

DATING & SEX

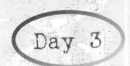

Understand That Premarital Sex Is Wrong

But because sexual sin is a danger,
each man should have his own wife,
and each woman should have her own husband.

1 CORINTHIANS 7:2 NCV

The fact that you're reading these words means that you're concerned about the issue of abstinence—and you should be. You live in a society that is filled to the brim with temptations, distractions, and distortions about sex. You are bombarded with images that glamorize sex outside marriage. In fact, you are subjected to new pressures and problems that were largely unknown to earlier generations. And at every corner, or so it seems, you are confronted with the message that premarital sex is a harmless activity, something that should be considered "recreational." That message is a terrible lie with tragic consequences.

God has a plan for your life, a plan that does not include sex before marriage. So do yourself a favor: wait. Abstinence is a choice: your choice. Please choose wisely.

2 minutes A DAY

more stuff to think about

The Bible has a word to describe "safe" sex.
It's called marriage.

GARY SMALLEY & JOHN TRENT

Your thoughts are the determining factor as to whose mold
you are conformed to. Control your thoughts and
you control the direction of your life.

CHARLES STANLEY

To many, total abstinence is easier than perfect moderation.

ST. AUGUSTINE

The Big Idea

If you're thinking about having sex before marriage, then
you should also think long and hard about the options you'll
have if you become pregnant or get someone else pregnant.
The best time to think about the responsibilities of being a
parent is before you get the results of the pregnancy test, not
after. And, if thinking about those options leaves you with a
sick feeling in the pit of your stomach, then don't have sex
until you're married.

DATING & SEX

Don't Overestimate the Importance of Cars, Clothes, and Other Stuff

He who trusts in his riches will fall,
but the righteous will flourish . . . .
PROVERBS 11:28 NKJV

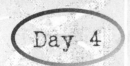

A re you overly impressed with stuff and money? If so, you may be setting yourself up for some unhappy relationships.

Our society is in love with money and the things that money can buy. God is not, and you shouldn't be, either.

If you find yourself wrapped up in the concerns of the material world, it's time to reorder your priorities by turning your thoughts to more important matters. And, it's time to begin storing up riches that will endure throughout eternity: the spiritual kind.

Money, in and of itself, is not evil; worshipping money is. So today, as you prioritize matters of importance in your life—and matters that pertain to your dating life—remember that God is almighty, but the dollar is not.

We are made spiritually lethargic
by a steady diet of materialism.

MARY MORRISON SUGGS

As faithful stewards of what we have, ought we not to give
earnest thought to our staggering surplus?

ELISABETH ELLIOT

Here's a simple test: If you can see it, it's not going to last.
The things that last are the things you cannot see.

DENNIS SWANBERG

The Big Idea

Too Much Stuff: Too much stuff doesn't ensure happiness.
In fact, having too much stuff can actually prevent
happiness.

DATING & SEX

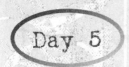

Don't Try to Please People, Try to Please God

Do you think I am trying to make people accept me?
No, God is the One I am trying to please.
Am I trying to please people? If I still wanted to
please people, I would not be a servant of Christ.
GALATIANS 1:10 NCV

Sometimes, it's very tempting to be a people-pleaser. But usually, it's the wrong thing to do.

When you worry too much about pleasing dates or friends, you may not worry enough about pleasing God—and when you fail to please God, you inevitably pay a very high price for your mistaken priorities.

Whom will you try to please today: God or your friends? Your obligation is most certainly not to your peers or to your date. Your obligation is to an all-knowing and perfect God. Trust Him always. Love Him always. Praise Him always. And seek to please Him and only Him. Always.

2 minutes A DAY

more stuff to think about

Never be afraid of the world's censure;
its praise is much more to be dreaded.

C. H. SPURGEON

People who constantly, and fervently, seek the approval of
others live with an identity crisis. They don't know who they
are, and they are defined by what others think of them.

CHARLES STANLEY

Every day, I find countless opportunities to decide
whether I will obey God and demonstrate my love for Him
or try to please myself or the world system.
God is waiting for my choices.

BILL BRIGHT

The Big Idea

If you are burdened with a "people-pleasing" personality,
outgrow it. Realize that you can't please all of the people all
of the time (including your dates), nor should you attempt to.

DATING & SEX

First, Focus on the Spiritual Stuff

For those whose lives are according to the flesh think about the things of the flesh, but those whose lives are according to the Spirit, about the things of the Spirit.

ROMANS 8:5 HOLMAN CSB

Is Christ the focus of your life? Are you fired with enthusiasm for Him? Are you an energized Christian who allows God's Son to reign over every aspect of your day? Make no mistake: that's exactly what God intends for you to do.

God has given you the gift of eternal life through His Son. In response to God's priceless gift, you are instructed to focus your thoughts, your prayers, and your energies upon God and His only begotten Son. To do so, you must resist the subtle yet powerful temptation to become a "spiritual dabbler."

A person who dabbles in the Christian faith is unwilling to place God in His rightful place: above all other things. Resist that temptation; make God the cornerstone and the touchstone of your life—including your dating life. When you do, He will give you all the strength and wisdom you need to live victoriously for Him.

more stuff to think about

Whatever we focus on determines what we become.

E. STANLEY JONES

Blessed are those who know what on earth they are
here on earth to do and set themselves about
the business of doing it.

MAX LUCADO

Jesus. If you are walking toward him to the best of your
ability, he will see you through life's unpredictable waters—
but you must risk launching the boat.

PATSY CLAIRMONT

The Big Idea

First focus on God . . . and then everything else will come
into focus.

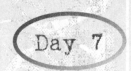

Insist Upon Shared Values

Be on guard. Stand true to what you believe.
Be courageous. Be strong.

1 CORINTHIANS 16:13 NLT

Is God a part of your dating life? Hopefully so. If you sincerely want to know God, then you should date people who feel the same way.

If you're still searching for Mr. or Mrs. Right (while trying to avoid falling in love with Mr. or Mrs. Wrong), be patient, be prudent, and be picky. Look for someone whose values you respect, whose behavior you approve of, and whose faith you admire. Remember that appearances can be deceiving and tempting, so watch your step. And when it comes to the important task of building a lifetime relationship with the guy or girl of your dreams, pray about it!

If you happen to be one of those very lucky ones who has already fallen madly in love with the same wonderful person who has (praise the Lord!) already fallen madly in love with you, say a great big thanks to the Matchmaker in heaven. But if you haven't yet found a soul-mate who honors both you and God, don't fret. Just keep trusting your Father in heaven, and keep yourself open to the direction in which He is leading you. And remember: When it comes to your dating life, God wants to give His approval—or not—but He won't give it until He's asked. So ask, listen, and decide accordingly.

more stuff to think about

Sadly, family problems and even financial problems are seldom the real problem, but often the symptom of a weak or nonexistent value system.

DAVE RAMSEY

As the first community to which a person is attached and the first authority under which a person learns to live, the family established society's most basic values.

CHARLES COLSON

The Big Idea

Look beyond appearances: Judging other people solely by appearances is tempting, but it's foolish, shortsighted, immature, and ultimately destructive. So don't do it.

DATING & SEX

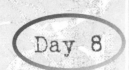

Remember: Cooperation Builds Relationships

Work at getting along with each other and with God. Otherwise you'll never get so much as a glimpse of God.

HEBREWS 12:14 MSG

Are you dating someone who understands the importance of cooperation? Or are you seeing someone who's more self-centered than that? And before you answer, here's something to consider: happy couples learn the wisdom of "give and take," not the foolishness of "me first."

Cooperative relationships flourish over time—one-sided relationships don't. So if you're dating someone who says, "It's my way or the highway," choose the highway. And choose it now.

more stuff to think about

Before God changes our circumstances,
He wants to change our hearts.

WARREN WIERSBE

Teamwork makes the dream work.

JOHN MAXWELL

Cooperation is a two-way street,
but for too many couples, it's the road less traveled.

MARIE T. FREEMAN

The Big Idea

If you're dating someone who doesn't consider your feelings,
you're dating the wrong person.

DATING & SEX

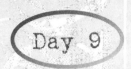
Decide How Far Is Too Far (And Stand Firm by Your Decision)

All who indulge in a sinful life are dangerously lawless, for sin is a major disruption of God's order.

1 JOHN 3:4 MSG

How far is too far? It's a question that lots of people ask themselves, and you probably will, too. And to discover the answer, think about it like this: the Bible teaches that your body isn't just a body, it's a temple—God's temple. And if you're dating a person who won't keep their hands to themselfs, they're trying to trash that temple. Don't let them do it!

And remember: it's not okay to trash the temple "just a little bit"—don't trash it at all! Father's order.

2 minutes a day

more stuff to think about

Integrity is the glue that holds our way of life together. We must constantly strive to keep our integrity intact. When wealth is lost, nothing is lost; when health is lost, something is lost; when character is lost, all is lost.

BILLY GRAHAM

Repentance is a complete surrender of my sinfulness to the only One who can cleanse me from all sin, and that is Jesus Christ.

ELISABETH ELLIOT

Sin is in the world. And sin is "missing the mark," missing God's perfect plan. There is so much of this missing the mark that it is going to impinge on every person's life at some points.

CATHERINE MARSHALL

The Big Idea

The time to decide how far is too far is long before you go out on a date—not during the date!

DATING & SEX

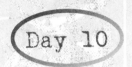

Day 10

Use God's Word as the Guide for Your Relationships

All Scripture is inspired by God and is profitable for teaching,
for rebuking, for correcting, for training in righteousness,
so that the man of God may be complete,
equipped for every good work.

2 Timothy 3:16-17 Holman CSB

I f you'd like to know what God has to say about your relationships, here's how you can find out. Read the book He wrote—it's called the Bible and it has timeless advice for life here on earth and life eternal.

The Bible is unlike any other book. It is a priceless gift from your Creator, a tool that God intends for you to use in every aspect of your life. And, it contains promises upon which you, as a Christian, can and must depend.

God's Word can be a roadmap to successful relationships and spiritual abundance. Make it your roadmap. God's wisdom can be a light to guide your steps. Claim it as your light today, tomorrow, and every day of your life—and then walk confidently in the footsteps of God's only begotten Son.

more stuff to think about

You may as well quit reading and hearing the Word of God,
and give it to the devil, if you do not desire
to live according to it.

MARTIN LUTHER

God can see clearly no matter how dark or foggy
the night is. Trust His Word to guide you safely home.

LISA WHELCHEL

It takes calm, thoughtful, prayerful meditation on
the Word to extract its deepest nourishment.

VANCE HAVNER

The Big Idea

Make Bible study a team sport. When two people study the
Word together, God blesses them and their relationship.

DATING & SEX

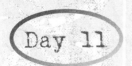

Listen Carefully to Your Conscience

Let us come near to God with a sincere heart and a sure faith, because we have been made free from a guilty conscience, and our bodies have been washed with pure water.

HEBREWS 10:22 NCV

Billy Graham correctly observed, "Most of us follow our conscience as we follow a wheelbarrow. We push it in front of us in the direction we want to go." To do so, of course, is a profound mistake. Yet all of us, on occasion, have failed to listen to the voice that God planted in our hearts, and all of us have suffered the consequences.

God gave you a conscience for a very good reason: to make your path conform to His will. Wise believers make it a practice to listen carefully to that quiet internal voice. Count yourself among that number. When your conscience speaks, listen and learn. In all likelihood, God is trying to get His message through. And in all likelihood, it is a message that you desperately need to hear.

2 minutes A DAY

To go against one's conscience is neither safe nor right.
Here I stand. I cannot do otherwise.

MARTIN LUTHER

The convicting work of the Holy Spirit awakens,
disturbs, and judges.

FRANKLIN GRAHAM

A good conscience is a continual feast.

FRANCIS BACON

The Big Idea

The more important the decision . . . the more carefully you
should listen to your conscience.

DATING & SEX

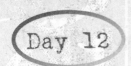

Always Treat Your Body with Respect

*Don't you know that you are God's temple
and that God's Spirit lives in you?*

1 CORINTHIANS 3:16 NCV

How do you treat your body? Do you treat it with the reverence and respect it deserves, or do you take it more or less for granted? Well, the Bible has clear instructions about the way you should take care of the miraculous body that God has given you.

God's Word teaches us that our bodies are "temples" which belong to God. We are commanded (not encouraged, not advised—commanded!) to treat our bodies with respect and honor. We do so by making wise choices and by making those choices consistently over an extended period of time.

Are you willing to treat your body with the reverence that it deserves? Then promise yourself—and God—that you will make the kind of wise choices that reflect your obedience to God's commandments. The responsibility for those choices is yours. And so are the rewards.

2 minutes A DAY

more stuff to think about

Our body is a portable sanctuary through which
we are daily experiencing the presence of God.

RICHARD FOSTER

People are funny. When they are young, they will spend
their health to get wealth. Later, they will gladly pay
all they have trying to get their health back.

JOHN MAXWELL

God wants you to give Him your body.
Some people do foolish things with their bodies.
God wants your body as a holy sacrifice.

WARREN WIERSBE

The Big Idea

God needs you, and He's given you a marvelous gift: your
body. Treat it marvelously.

DATING & SEX

Trust God's Plans

You will teach me how to live a holy life.
Being with you will fill me with joy;
at your right hand I will find pleasure forever.

PSALM 16:11 NCV

The Bible makes it clear: God's got a plan—a very big plan—and you're an important part of that plan. But here's the catch: God won't force His plans upon you; you've got to figure things out for yourself . . . or not.

As a follower of Christ, you should ask yourself this question: "How closely can I make my plans match God's plans?" The more closely you manage to follow the path that God intends for your life, the better.

Do you have questions or concerns about your relationships? Take them to God in prayer. Do you have hopes and expectations? Talk to God about your dreams. Are you carefully planning for the days and weeks ahead? Consult God as you establish your priorities. Turn every concern over to your Heavenly Father, and sincerely seek His guidance—prayerfully, earnestly, and often. Then, listen for His answers . . . and trust the answers that He gives.

more stuff to think about

God possesses infinite knowledge and awareness which is uniquely His. At all times, even in the midst of any type of suffering, I can realize that he knows, loves, watches, understands, and more than that, He has a purpose.

BILLY GRAHAM

I don't doubt that the Holy Spirit guides your decisions from within when you make them with the intention of pleasing God. The error would be to think that He speaks only within, whereas in reality He speaks also through Scripture, the Church, Christian friends, and books.

C. S. LEWIS

The God who orchestrates the universe has a good many things to consider that have not occurred to me, and it is well that I leave them to Him.

ELISABETH ELLIOT

The Big Idea

When life seems unfair, try spending more time trusting God and less time dwelling on "the unfairness of it all."

DATING & SEX

Be Forewarned: Dishonesty and Immorality Eat Away at Your Heart, Your Soul, and Your Relationships

*The righteousness of the blameless clears his path,
but the wicked person will fall because of his wickedness.*

PROVERBS 11:5 HOLMAN CSB

When you become involved in relationships that require you to compromise your values, you'll make yourself miserable. Why? Because God has given you a conscience that tells you right from wrong, that's why.

It has been said that character is what you are when nobody is watching. How true. But, as Bill Hybels correctly observed, "Every secret act of character, conviction, and courage has been observed in living color by our omniscient God." And isn't that a sobering thought?

If you sincerely wish to walk with God, you must seek, to the best of your ability, to follow His commandments. When you do, your character will take care of itself . . . and you won't need to look over your shoulder to see who, besides God, is watching.

more stuff to think about

God's presence is such a cleansing fire,
confession and repentance are always there.

ANNE ORTLUND

The great test of a man's character is his tongue.

OSWALD CHAMBERS

God cannot build character without our cooperation.
If we resist Him, then He chastens us into submission.
But, if we submit to Him, then He can accomplish His work.
He is not satisfied with a halfway job. God wants
a perfect work; He wants a finished product
that is mature and complete.

WARREN WIERSBE

The Big Idea

Never accept blatant dishonesty as a part of any
relationship, and never accept physical or emotional abuse
from anyone, especially those people who are closest to you.

DATING & SEX

Don't Make Impulsive Decisions That Might Affect the Rest of Your Life

*Happy is the person who finds wisdom,
the one who gets understanding.*
PROVERBS 3:13 NCV

The decision to have sex before you're married—or the decision to abstain from it—is a choice that will most certainly impact the rest of your life. That decision will play an important role in the way you see yourself, and it will play an important role in the way you view relationships with members of the opposite sex. And of course, there's always the chance that your decision to have sex might result in an unexpected "surprise."

Face it: there's a lot riding on the decision to abstain from sex. And because it's an important decision, you should think about it—and pray about it—before you make a decision that might just change the direction of your life.

As you're making up your mind about the role that sex will play in your life, trust the quiet inner voice of your conscience, and be obedient to the teaching you find in God's Word. When you do, you'll make the right decision . . . and you'll be eternally grateful that you did.

more stuff to think about

Very few things motivate us to give God
our undivided attention like being faced with
the negative consequences of our decisions.

CHARLES STANLEY

Wisdom is the right use of knowledge.
To know is not to be wise. Many men know a great deal,
and are all the greater fools for it. But to know how
to use knowledge is to have wisdom.

C. H. SPURGEON

The fruit of wisdom is Christlikeness, peace, humility,
and love. And, the root of it is faith in Christ
as the manifested wisdom of God.

J. I. PACKER

The Big Idea

Put the brakes on impulsive behavior . . . before impulsive
behavior puts the brakes on you.

DATING & SEX

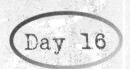

Understand that Promiscuity Is a Terrible Way to Build a Lasting Relationship

*Though I speak with the tongues of men and of angels,
but have not love, I have become sounding brass
or a clanging cymbal.*

1 CORINTHIANS 13:1 NKJV

If you're trying to build a relationship based only on physical attraction, you'll be disappointed. Lasting relationships aren't built upon lust, they're built upon love—real love.

How do you define love? Hopefully, you understand that it's something more than physical attraction. Genuine love is patient, understanding, consistent, and considerate. Genuine love doesn't just sit around and do nothing; it gets translated into acts of kindness—both large and small.

Love is always a choice. Sometimes, of course, we may "fall in love," but it takes work to stay there. Sometimes, we may be "swept off our feet," but the "sweeping" is only temporary; sooner or later, if love is to endure, one must plant one's feet firmly on the ground. The decision to love another person for a lifetime is much more than the simple process of "falling in" or "being swept up." It requires "reaching out," "holding firm," and "lifting up." Love, then, becomes a decision to honor and care for the other person, come what may.

more stuff to think about

Let no one tell you that this body of ours is
a stranger to God.

ST. CYRIL OF JERUSALEM

The best use of life is love.
The best expression of love is time.
The best time to love is now.

RICK WARREN

The Big Idea

Sex can wait: If you're really serious about this person, and if you're really serious about putting God first, then it's worth the wait.

DATING & SEX

See Through the Media's Distorted Messages About Sex

Do not love the world or the things in the world.
If you love the world, the love of the Father is not in you.

1 JOHN 2:15 NCV

Sometimes it's hard being a Christian, especially when the world keeps pumping out messages that are contrary to your faith.

The media is working around the clock in an attempt to rearrange your priorities. The media says that your appearance is all-important, that your clothes are all-important, that partying is all-important, and that sex should be "recreational." But guess what? Those messages are lies. Period. And those messages can hurt you.

So, the next time you're attacked by a pack of 21st-century media lies, don't be taken in. Forget the media hype, and pay attention to God. You owe it to God . . . and you owe it to yourself.

more stuff to think about

Some of the most ordinary looking women imaginable by the world's standards possess a beauty that is utterly striking because of the condition of their hearts.

ED YOUNG

Fashion is an enduring testimony to the fact that we live quite consciously before the eyes of others.

JOHN ELDREDGE

The problem is that the culture seeps into the church, bringing with it a religion without commitment; spirituality without content; aspiration and talk and longing, fulfillment and needs, but not much concern about God.

EUGENE PETERSON

The Big Idea

Don't trust the media's messages! Many of the messages that you receive from the media are specifically designed to sell you products that interfere with your spiritual, physical, or emotional health. God takes great interest in your health; the moguls from Madison Avenue take great interest in your pocketbook. Trust God.

DATING & SEX

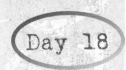

Don't Be Afraid to Ask Him for Help

And yet the reason you don't have what you want is that you don't ask God for it.

JAMES 4:2 NLT

If you want to know more about your relationships, ask God for His help! When you ask sincerely—and repeatedly—He will answer your request.

How often do you ask God for His guidance and His wisdom? Occasionally? Intermittently? Whenever you experience a crisis? Hopefully not. Hopefully, you've acquired the habit of asking for God's assistance early and often. And hopefully, you have learned to seek His guidance in every aspect of your life.

more stuff to think about

We get into trouble when we think we know
what to do and we stop asking God if we're doing it.

STORMIE OMARTIAN

Notice that we must ask. And we will sometimes struggle
to hear and struggle with what we hear. But personally,
it's worth it. I'm after the path of life—and he alone knows it.

JOHN ELDREDGE

When you ask God to do something, don't ask timidly;
put your whole heart into it.

MARIE T. FREEMAN

The Big Idea

If you want more from life, ask more from God. If you're
seeking a worthy goal, ask for God's help—and keep
asking—until He answers your prayers.

DATING & SEX

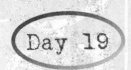

Understand That Premarital Sex Can Be Profoundly Damaging to Your Emotional Health

Run away from infantile indulgence.
Run after mature righteousness—faith, love, peace—
joining those who are in honest and
serious prayer before God.
2 TIMOTHY 2:22 MSG

Premarital sex isn't just dangerous to your spiritual health, it's also dangerous to emotional health. If you compromise your values by disobeying God's laws, sooner or later your conscience will punish you for it—and probably sooner rather than later.

Emotional health is contagious, and so is emotional distress. If you're fortunate enough to be dating someone who obeys God and respects you, consider yourself profoundly blessed. But, if you find yourself caught in an unhealthy relationship, it's time to look realistically at your situation and begin making changes . . . now!

2 MINUTES A DAY

Be half a Christian, and you will have just enough
religion to make you miserable.

C. H. SPURGEON

When we do what is right, we have contentment,
peace, and happiness.

BEVERLY LAHAYE

We must appropriate the tender mercy of God every day
after conversion, or problems quickly develop.
We need his grace daily in order to live a righteous life.

JIM CYMBALA

The Big Idea

Find the right crowd and join it. And while you're at it, avoid
people and places that might tempt you to disobey God's
commandments.

DATING & SEX

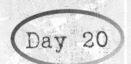

Day 20

Keep Your Priorities in Line with God's Priorities

Come near to God, and God will come near to you.
You sinners, clean sin out of your lives. You who are trying to
follow God and the world at the same time,
make your thinking pure.

JAMES 4:8 NCV

Have you fervently asked God to help prioritize Your life? Have you asked Him for guidance and for the courage to do the things that you know need to be done? If so, then you're continually inviting your Creator to reveal Himself in a variety of ways. As a follower of Christ, you must do no less.

When you make God's priorities your priorities, you will receive God's abundance and His peace. When you make God a full partner in every aspect of your life, He will lead you along the proper path: His path. When you allow God to reign over your heart, He will honor you with spiritual blessings that are simply too numerous to count. So, as you build your relationships and live your life, make God's will your ultimate priority. When you do, every other priority will have a tendency to fall neatly into place.

2 minutes A DAY

A disciple is a follower of Christ. That means you take on His priorities as your own. His agenda becomes your agenda. His mission becomes your mission.

CHARLES STANLEY

God is everything. My focus must be on him, seeking to know him more completely and allowing Him full possession of my life.

MARY MORRISON SUGGS

Sin is largely a matter of mistaken priorities. Any sin in us that is cherished, hidden, and not confessed will cut the nerve center of our faith.

CATHERINE MARSHALL

The Big Idea

Setting priorities may mean saying no . . . You don't have time to do everything, so it's perfectly okay to say no the things that mean less so that you'll have time for the things that mean more.

DATING & SEX

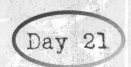

Understand This:
Everybody Isn't Doing It

Don't become partners with those who reject God.
How can you make a partnership out of right and wrong?
That's not partnership; that's war.
Is light best friends with dark?

2 CORINTHIANS 6:14 MSG

Perhaps you have friends who boast about sex. If so, it may seem to you that "everybody is doing it." But they're not. In fact, millions of young adults know that premarital sex is just plain wrong. And you must understand it, too.

When you think about it, the argument in favor of abstinence isn't a very hard case to make. First and foremost, abstinence is a part of God's plan for people who are not married. Period. But it doesn't stop there: abstinence is also the right thing to do and the smart thing to do.

If you're involved with people who try to convince you that it's okay to have sex before marriage, you're hanging out with the wrong people. So do yourself a favor: find friends who know that everybody isn't doing it . . . because they aren't!

more stuff to think about

I hope you will find a few folks who walk with God
to also walk with you through the seasons of your life.

JOHN ELDREDGE

It is comfortable to know that we are responsible
to God and not to man. It is a small matter
to be judged of man's judgement.

LOTTIE MOON

I have found that the closer I am to the godly people
around me, the easier it is for me to live a righteous life
because they hold me accountable.

JOHN MACARTHUR

The Big Idea

Put peer pressure to work for you: How? By associating with
people who, by their actions and their words, will encourage
you to become a better person.

DATING & SEX

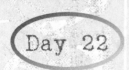

Treat Mind-altering Substances Like Poison (Because That's What They Are!)

*Be sober! Be on the alert! Your adversary
the Devil is prowling around like a roaring lion,
looking for anyone he can devour.*

1 Peter 5:8 Holman CSB

Do you hang out with people who consider "partying" to be the most important aspect of their lives? If so, you're headed headlong down a dead-end street . . . right along with your friends.

Mind-altering substances (including the most popular American mind-bender of all: good old-fashioned beer) are dangerous . . . make that Dangerous (with a capital D).

So here are three things to remember about alcohol and other drugs: 1. If you're drinking or drugging, you must either stop that behavior or face very disastrous consequences. 2. If you're spending time with people who think that alcohol and drugs are "harmless," you're choosing to associate with some very naïve people. 3. If you're dating someone who drinks or drugs, you deserve better . . . much better. End of lecture.

2 minutes a day

more stuff to think about

To many, total abstinence is easier than perfect moderation.

ST. AUGUSTINE

Addiction is the most powerful psychic enemy
of humanity's desire for God.

GERALD MAY

Whatever you love most, be it sports, pleasure,
business or God, that is your god.

BILLY GRAHAM

The Big Idea

Make Jesus your highest priority, and ask Him to help you
overcome any behaviors that might distance you from Him.

DATING & SEX

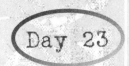

Remember: If You Wait, You'll Always Be Glad (And If You Don't You'll Always Regret It)

Those who obey his commands live in him, and he in them.
And this is how we know that he lives in us:
We know it by the Spirit he gave us.

1 JOHN 3:24 NIV

If you choose to have sex before you're married, you're going to regret it. And you're not going to stop regretting it any time soon. In fact, the decision to become sexually active is such a big decision that you'll probably keep thinking about it for the rest of your life. So do yourself a huge favor: don't dare disobey God—abstain from sex until you say, "I do!"

Whenever you commit a sin, God will forgive you when you ask Him—but you may have a much harder time forgiving yourself. So the best way to avoid a lifetime of regrets is to listen to your conscience and obey your Father in heaven. When you do, you won't regret it.

2 minutes a day

more stuff to think about

We are always making an offering.
If we do not give to God, we give to the devil.

VANCE HAVNER

God's love for His children is unconditional, no strings
attached. But, God's blessings on our lives do come
with a condition—obedience. If we are to receive
the fullness of God's blessings, we must obey Him
and keep His commandments.

JIM GALLERY

It takes faith to obey God,
but God always rewards obedient faith.

WARREN WIERSBE

The Big Idea

Obedience leads to spiritual growth: Anne Graham Lotz
correctly observed, "If you want to discover your spiritual
gifts, start obeying God. As you serve Him, you will find
that He has given you the gifts that are necessary to follow
through in obedience."

DATING & SEX

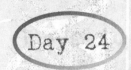

Day 24

Build Relationships That Will Last

And regardless of what else you put on, wear love.
It's your basic, all-purpose garment. Never be without it.
Let the peace of Christ keep you in tune with each other,
in step with each other. None of this going off and doing
your own thing. And cultivate thankfulness.

COLOSSIANS 3:14-15 MSG

D o you want to build a relationship that lasts? Then you must start by making God the cornerstone of your relationships.

God does not intend for you to experience mediocre relationships; He created you for far greater things. Building lasting relationships requires compassion, wisdom, empathy, kindness, courtesy, and forgiveness (lots of forgiveness). If that sounds a lot like work, it is—which is perfectly fine with God. Why? Because He knows that you are capable of doing that work, and because He knows that the fruits of your labors will enrich the lives of your loved ones and the lives of generations yet unborn.

2 MINUTES A DAY

Living life with a consistent spiritual walk
deeply influences those we love most.

VONETTE BRIGHT

Healthy relationships include laughter. Every relationship,
whether it is with your spouse or your children,
can be filled with joy and with laughter.

DENNIS SWANBERG

Line by line, moment by moment, special times are
etched into our memories in the permanent ink of
everlasting love in our relationships.

GLORIA GAITHER

The Big Idea

Communication is vital to the health of any relationship. If
you're having trouble expressing yourself, don't clam up.
Instead, keep trying until you finally get the hang of it.

DATING & SEX

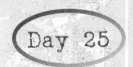

If Things Get Serious, Be Involved (Together) in Church

*For we are laborers together with God:
ye are God's husbandry, ye are God's building.*

1 CORINTHIANS 3:9 KJV

I f you become involved in a serious relationship, it's time for the two of you to start discussing your faith. And it's probably time to start attending church together.

We live in a world that is teeming with temptations and distractions—a world where good and evil struggle in a constant battle to win our hearts and souls. Our challenge, of course, is to ensure that we cast our lot on the side of God. One way to ensure that we do so is by the practice of regular, purposeful worship. When we worship God faithfully and fervently, we are blessed. When we fail to worship God, for whatever reason, we forfeit the spiritual gifts that He intends for us.

Every day provides opportunities to put God where He belongs: at the center of our lives and our relationships. When we do so, we worship not just with our words, but also with deeds, and that's as it should be. For believers, God comes first. Always first.

more stuff to think about

Christians are like coals of a fire.
Together they glow—apart they grow cold.

QUIPS, ANONYMOUS

And if our fellowship below in Jesus be so sweet,
what greater blessings shall we know when
'round His throne we meet?

CHARLES WESLEY

One of the ways God refills us after failure is through
the blessing of Christian fellowship. Just experiencing
the joy of simple activities shared with other children of God
can have a healing effect on us.

ANNE GRAHAM LOTZ

The Big Idea

Here is a short list of things God wants you and your friends
to do: 1. Go to church. 2. Pay attention in church 3. Support
the church. 4. Enjoy the fellowship of the people you meet in
church. End of sermon.

DATING & SEX

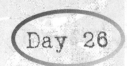

Don't Overestimate the Importance of Appearances

As the water reflects the face, so the heart reflects the person.
PROVERBS 27:19 HOLMAN CSB

The world sees you as you appear to be; God sees you as you really are. He sees your heart, and He understands your intentions. The opinions of others should be relatively unimportant to you; however, God's view of you—His understanding of your actions, your thoughts, and your motivations—should be vitally important.

Few things in life are more futile than "keeping up appearances" in order to impress your friends and your dates—yet the media would have you believe otherwise. The media would have you believe that everything depends on the color of your hair, the condition of your wardrobe, and the model of the car you drive. But nothing could be further from the truth. What is important, of course, is pleasing your Father in heaven. You please Him when your intentions are pure and your actions are just. When you do, you will be blessed today, tomorrow, and forever.

2 minutes A DAY

more stuff to think about

God doesn't use us based on what we look like.
He uses us based on the condition of our souls.

JUDITH COUCHMAN

Outside appearances, things like the clothes you wear or the
car you drive, are important to other people
but totally unimportant to God. Trust God.

MARIE T. FREEMAN

If the narrative of the Scriptures teaches us anything, from
the serpent in the Garden to the carpenter in Nazareth,
it teaches us that things are rarely what they seem,
that we shouldn't be fooled by appearances.

JOHN ELDREDGE

The Big Idea

When making judgments about friends and dates, don't
focus on appearances, focus on values.

DATING & SEX

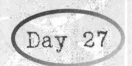

Pray About It!

*If you don't know what you're doing, pray to the Father.
He loves to help. You'll get his help, and won't be
condescended to when you ask for it. Ask boldly, believingly,
without a second thought. People who "worry their prayers"
are like wind-whipped waves. Don't think you're going
to get anything from the Master that way, adrift at sea,
keeping all your options open.*

JAMES 1:5-8 MSG

O h, how glorious are the dreams of love—but oh
how tough it is to turn those dreams into reality!
If you're still searching for Mr. or Miss Right,
be patient, be prudent, and be picky. Look for a person
whose values you respect, whose behavior you approve of,
and whose faith you admire. Remember that appearances
can be deceiving and tempting, so watch your step. And
when it comes to the important task of building a lifetime
relationship with the guy or girl of your dreams, pray about
it! God is waiting to give His approval—or not—but He
won't give it until He's asked. So ask, listen, and decide
accordingly.

2 minutes a day

more stuff to think about

Even more than we long to be heard, God desires to listen.

Angela Thomas

Where there is much prayer, there will be much of the Spirit;
where there is much of the Spirit,
there will be ever-increasing power.

Andrew Murray

He who is his own guide is guided by a fool.

C. H. Spurgeon

The Big Idea

Sometimes, the answer to prayer is "No." God doesn't grant all of our requests, nor should He. We must understand that our prayers are answered by a sovereign, all-knowing God, and that we must trust His answers.

DATING & SEX

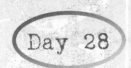

Learn How to Deal with Rejection

I've told you all this so that trusting me, you will be unshakable and assured, deeply at peace. In this godless world you will continue to experience difficulties. But take heart! I've conquered the world.

JOHN 16:33 MSG

Sometimes, you may feel pressured to compromise yourself, and you may be afraid of what will happen if you firmly say "No." You may be afraid that you'll be rejected. But here's a tip: don't worry too much about rejection, especially when you're rejected for doing the right thing.

Pleasing other people is a good thing . . . up to a point. But you must never allow your "willingness to please" to interfere with your own good judgement or with God's commandments.

Instead of being afraid of rejection, focus on pleasing your Creator first and always. And when it comes to the world and all its inhabitants, don't worry too much about the folks you can't please. Focus, instead, on doing the right thing—and leave the rest up to God.

more stuff to think about

When you taste a measure of being able to love and enjoy the people in your life, without having to have any particular response from them, you are tasting bliss.

PAULA RINEHART

A healthy self-identity is seeing yourself as God sees you— no more and no less.

JOSH MCDOWELL

Confidence in the natural world is self-reliance; in the spiritual world, it is God-reliance.

OSWALD CHAMBERS

The Big Idea

If you have a choice between pleasing people and pleasing God . . . please God!

DATING & SEX

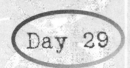

Insist Upon
Mutual Respect

Here is a simple, rule-of-thumb for behavior:
Ask yourself what you want people to do for you,
then grab the initiative and do it for them.
Add up God's Law and Prophets and this is what you get.

MATTHEW 7:12 MSG

D o you respect yourself enough to demand that your dates respect you, too? Please, please, please answer that question with a resounding YES! Why? Because if you don't respect yourself, other people (including, but not limited to members of the opposite sex) may find it easy to take advantage of you.

Think about it like this: the more you respect yourself, the more likely you are to make smart decisions . . . and the smarter decisions you make, the more reasons you'll have to respect yourself—it's a cycle of good decision making that reinforces a well-deserved, positive self-image.

But what if you find that your self-image could use a tune-up? Well, try these five simple steps: 1. Don't do things that you know to be immoral, imprudent, or impulsive. 2. Make the conscious effort to invest yourself in activities that improve your own life and the lives of others. 3. If you're

2 minutes A DAY

beset by negative self-talk, put an immediate stop to the mindless ramblings of your inner critic. 4. Associate yourself with people who encourage you to think and behave in ways that are pleasing to God. 5. Ask your Heavenly Father to guide your path and direct your thoughts.

When you take these simple steps, you'll respect yourself more, and you'll demand the same kind of respect from the people you date.

more stuff to think about

We can be secure in the knowledge that our value and worth are not dependent upon who we are or what we think or say or do. It is based on who we are in Christ Jesus.

JOYCE MEYER

If you are willing to honor a person out of respect for God, you can be assured that God will honor you.

BETH MOORE

The Big Idea

Be choosy: Don't "settle" for second-class treatment—you deserve someone who values you as a person . . . and shows it.

DATING & SEX

Real Worship Requires Obedience

*God is spirit, and those who worship him
must worship in spirit and truth.*

JOHN 4:24 NCV

All of mankind is engaged in the practice of worship.
Some people choose to worship God and, as a
result, reap the joy that He intends for His children.
Others distance themselves from God by worshipping such
things as earthly possessions or personal gratification . . .
and when they do, they suffer.

What will you choose to worship today? Will you worship
your Creator or your possessions? Will you worship your
Savior, Jesus Christ, or will you bow down before the false
gods of pride and popularity? Will you seek the approval of
your God or the approval of your peers? Every day provides
opportunities to put God where He belongs: at the center of
your life. Worship Him—and only Him—today, tomorrow,
and always.

2 minutes A DAY

more stuff to think about

True faith commits us to obedience.

A. W. Tozer

Disobedience to His Word will cause you to doubt.

Anne Graham Lotz

Our obedience does not make God any bigger
or better than He already is. Anything God commands of us
is so that our joy may be full—the joy of seeing
His glory revealed to us and in us!

Beth Moore

The Big Idea

Obey God or face the consequences. God rewards
obedience and punishes disobedience. It's not enough to
understand God's rules; you must also live by them . . . or
else.

DATING & SEX

Hang Out with the Right Crowd

He that walketh with wise men shall be wise:
but a companion of fools shall be destroyed.

Proverbs 13:20 KJV

Some friends encourage you to obey God—these friends help you make wise choices. Other friends put you in situations where you are tempted to disobey God—these friends tempt you to make unwise choices.

Are you hanging out with—and dating—people who, by their presence and their influence, make you a better Christian? Or are you spending time with people who encourage you to stray from your faith? The answer to this question will help determine the condition of both your relationships and your spiritual health. One of the best ways to ensure that you follow Christ is to find fellow believers who are willing to follow Him with you. And if you can't find friends like that, you're looking in the wrong places.

2 minutes A DAY

more stuff to think about

You will get untold flak for prioritizing God's revealed
and present will for your life over man's . . .
but, boy, is it worth it.

BETH MOORE

We, as God's people, are not only to stay far away from sin
and sinners who would entice us, but we are to be
so like our God that we mourn over sin.

KAY ARTHUR

Those who follow the crowd usually get lost in it.

RICK WARREN

The Big Idea

If you want to meet new people, go to the places where you
are likely to bump into the kind of people you want to meet:
you probably won't find the right kind of person in the wrong
kind of place.

DATING & SEX

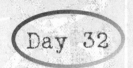

Day 32

Beware of Temptations

No temptation has seized you except what is common to man. And God is faithful; he will not let you be tempted beyond what you can bear. But when you are tempted, he will also provide a way out so that you can stand up under it.

1 CORINTHIANS 10:13 NIV

You've got to admit that you live in a temptation-filled world. The devil is hard at work in your neighborhood, and so are his helpers. Here in the 21st century, the bad guys are working around the clock to lead you astray. That's why you must remain vigilant.

In a letter to believers, Peter offers a stern warning: "Your adversary, the devil, prowls around like a roaring lion, seeking someone to devour" (1 Peter 5:8 NASB). What was true in New Testament times is equally true in our own. Satan tempts his prey and then devours them (and it's up to you—and only you—to make sure that you're not one of the ones being devoured!).

As a young adult in search of godly relationships, you must beware because temptations are everywhere. Satan is determined to win; you must be equally determined that he does not.

2 minutes A DAY

more stuff to think about

A Christian should no more defile his body
than a Jew would defile the temple.

WARREN WIERSBE

Above all, we must be especially alert against the beginnings
of temptation, for the enemy is more easily conquered
if he is refused admittance to the mind and is met
beyond the threshold when he knocks.

THOMAS À KEMPIS

Give Satan an inch and he'll be a ruler.

ANONYMOUS

The Big Idea

If life's inevitable temptations seem to be getting the best of
you, try praying more often, even if many of those prayers
are simply brief, "open-eyed" requests to your Father in
heaven.

DATING & SEX

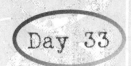

Be Hungry for Righteousness

Blessed are those who hunger and thirst for righteousness,
for they will be filled.

MATTHEW 5:6 NIV

D o you want to be a righteous person, and do you want to experience righteous relationships? Are you bound and determined—despite the inevitable temptations and distractions of our modern age—to be an example of godly behavior to your family and your friends? If so, you must "hunger and thirst" for righteousness. What, precisely, do the words "hunger and thirst" mean? Simply this: you must yearn to be righteous; you must strive to be righteous; and you must work to be righteous by putting aside many of the things that the world holds dear.

You will not become righteous by accident. You must hunger for righteousness, and when you do, you will be filled.

more stuff to think about

Have your heart right with Christ, and he will visit you often,
and so turn weekdays into Sundays, meals into sacraments,
homes into temples, and earth into heaven.

C. H. SPURGEON

Impurity is not just a wrong action; impurity is the state of
mind and heart and soul which is just the opposite
of purity and wholeness.

A. W. TOZER

Our souls were made to live in an upper atmosphere,
and we stifle and choke if we live on any lower level.
Our eyes were made to look off from these heavenly heights,
and our vision is distorted by any lower gazing.

HANNAH WHITALL SMITH

The Big Idea

The world's value system is flawed. God's value system is
not. Act accordingly.

DATING & SEX

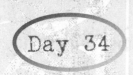

Be Disciplined

But I discipline my body and bring it into subjection,
lest, when I have preached to others,
I myself should become disqualified.

1 CORINTHIANS 9:27 NKJV

Are you a self-disciplined person? If so, congratulations . . . your disciplined approach to life can help you build a more meaningful relationship with God. Why? Because God expects all His believers (including you) to lead lives of disciplined obedience to Him . . . and He rewards those believers who do.

God doesn't reward laziness, misbehavior, or apathy. God is less concerned with your party time than He is with your prayer time. And God wants all His followers (including you) to behave with dignity and self-control. No exceptions.

So if you want to know God a little better, try becoming a more disciplined person. When you do, you'll be rewarded, richly rewarded, for your efforts.

more stuff to think about

Real freedom means to welcome the responsibility it brings,
to welcome the God-control it requires, to welcome the
discipline that results, to welcome the maturity it creates.

EUGENIA PRICE

Personal humility is a spiritual discipline and
the hallmark of the service of Jesus.

FRANKLIN GRAHAM

As we seek to become disciples of Jesus Christ,
we should never forget that the word *disciple* is directly
related to the word *discipline*. To be a disciple of
the Lord Jesus Christ is to know his discipline.

DENNIS SWANBERG

The Big Idea

A disciplined lifestyle gives you more control: The more
disciplined you become, the more you can take control over
your life (which, by the way, is far better than letting your life
take control over you).

DATING & SEX

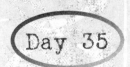

Look for Fulfillment in All the Right Places

I am the Gate. Anyone who goes through me will be cared for—will freely go in and out, and find pasture. A thief is only there to steal and kill and destroy. I came so they can have real and eternal life, more and better life than they ever dreamed of. I am the Good Shepherd. The Good Shepherd puts the sheep before himself, sacrifices himself if necessary.

JOHN 10:9-11 MSG

Where can we find fulfillment? Is it a result of money or popularity or looks or material possessions? Hardly. Genuine contentment is a gift from God to those who trust Him and follow His commandments.

Our world seems preoccupied with the search for happiness. We are bombarded with messages telling us that happiness depends upon the acquisition of more and more stuff. These messages are false.

If we don't find contentment in God, we will never find it anywhere else. But, if we seek Him and obey Him, we will be blessed with an inner peace that is beyond human understanding. When God dwells at the center of our lives, peace and contentment will belong to us just as surely as we belong to God.

more stuff to think about

We will never be happy until we make God the source
of our fulfillment and the answer to our longings.

STORMIE OMARTIAN

Regardless of how busy we become with all things Christian,
we must remember that the most transforming practice
available to us is the disciplined intake of Scripture.

DONALD S. WHITNEY

By trying to grab fulfillment everywhere, we find it nowhere.

ELISABETH ELLIOT

The Big Idea

First, focus on your relationship with God. Then, you'll find
that other relationships will be more fulfilling.

DATING & SEX

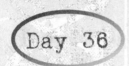

Be a Good Example

For am I now trying to win the favor of people, or God?
Or am I striving to please people?
If I were still trying to please people,
I would not be a slave of Christ.
GALATIANS 1:10 HOLMAN CSB

Whether you like it or not, you simply can't deny the fact that you're an example to other people. The question is not whether you will be an example to your family and friends; the question is precisely what kind of example will you be.

Corrie ten Boom advised, "Don't worry about what you do not understand. Worry about what you do understand in the Bible but do not live by." And that's sound advice because your family, friends, and dates are always watching ... and so, for that matter, is God.

2 minutes A DAY

more stuff to think about

Too many Christians have geared their program to please,
to entertain, and to gain favor from this world.
We are concerned with how much, instead of how little,
like this age we can become.

BILLY GRAHAM

Nothing speaks louder or more powerfully
than a life of integrity.

CHARLES SWINDOLL

In your desire to share the gospel,
you may be the only Jesus someone else will ever meet.
Be real and be involved with people.

BARBARA JOHNSON

The Big Idea

If you're a Christian, behave like one. The sermons you live
are far more important than the sermons you preach.

DATING & SEX

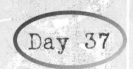

Remember This: If You're Feeling Too Much Pressure to Have Sex, You're Dating the Wrong Person (and It's Time to Break Things Off)

For God has not called us to impurity, but to sanctification.
1 THESSALONIANS 4:7 HOLMAN CSB

If you're seeing someone who's pressuring you to become sexually active, here's an important question to ask yourself: Why, in the name of common sense, would you want to date a person like that? After all, if the person you're dating really cares about you—and if that person wants to spend the rest of his or her life with you—waiting isn't really a sacrifice, it's an honor. But if the person you're dating simply views you as a sexual conquest, then you'd better run, run as fast as you can . . . in the opposite direction.

Common sense tells you to wait; God's Word commands you to wait; and your conscience begs you to wait. So wait! And if somebody tells you to do otherwise, you have absolutely no business dating them. Period.

2 minutes A DAY

more stuff to think about

Tell me what company you keep,
and I'll tell you what you are.

MIGUEL DE CERVANTES

A pure theology and a loose morality will never mix.

C. H. SPURGEON

Jesus gives us the ultimate rest, the confidence we need,
to escape the frustration and chaos of the world around us.

BILLY GRAHAM

The Big Idea

If you're feeling pressure from your date, it's time to end
your date.

DATING & SEX

Trust God's Promises

Patient endurance is what you need now,
so you will continue to do God's will.
Then you will receive all that he has promised.

HEBREWS 10:36 NLT

Want to improve your life and your relationships? Try paying a little more attention to God's promises. God has made quite a few promises to you, and He intends to keep every single one of them. You will find these promises in a book like no other: the Holy Bible. The Bible is your roadmap for life here on earth and for life eternal—as a believer, you are called upon to trust its promises, to follow its commandments, and to share its Good News.

God's promises never fail and they never grow old. You must trust those promises and share them with your friends, with your family, and with the world . . . starting now . . . and ending never.

2 minutes A DAY

more stuff to think about

There are four words I wish we would never forget,
and they are, "God keeps his word."

CHARLES SWINDOLL

The promises of Scripture are not mere pious hopes or
sanctified guesses. They are more than sentimental words to
be printed on decorated cards for Sunday School children.
They are eternal verities. They are true.
There is no perhaps about them.

PETER MARSHALL

We honor God by asking for great things when
they are a part of His promise. We dishonor Him and cheat
ourselves when we ask for molehills where
He has promised mountains.

VANCE HAVNER

The Big Idea

Do you really trust God's promises, or are you hedging your
bets? Today, think about the role that God's Word plays in
your life, and think about ways that you can worry less and
trust God more.

DATING & SEX

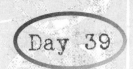

Share Your Testimony

*This and this only has been my appointed work:
getting this news to those who have never heard of God,
and explaining how it works by simple faith and plain truth.*

1 TIMOTHY 2:7 MSG

A good way to build your faith is by talking about it—to friends, to family members, to dates, and even to strangers—and that's precisely what God wants you to do.

Let's face facts: You live in a world that desperately needs the healing message of Jesus Christ. Every believer, including you, bears responsibility for sharing the Good News. And it is important to remember that you give your testimony through your words and your actions.

So today, preach the Gospel through your words and your deeds . . . but not necessarily in that order.

2 minutes A DAY

more stuff to think about

Kindness has converted more people than zeal,
science or eloquence.

MOTHER TERESA

Christianity spread rapidly during the first century because
all Christians saw themselves as responsible for
disseminating the gospel.

ERWIN LUTZER

There is nothing more appealing or convincing to
a watching world than to hear the testimony of
someone who has just been with Jesus.

HENRY BLACKABY

The Big Idea

Your Story Is Important: D. L. Moody, the famed evangelist
from Chicago, said, "Remember, a small light will do a
great deal when it is in a very dark place. Put one little tallow
candle in the middle of a large hall, and it will give a great
deal of light." Make certain that your candle is always lit.
Give your testimony, and trust God to do the rest.

DATING & SEX

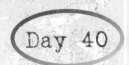

Live on Purpose

*God chose you to be his people, so I urge you now
to live the life to which God called you.*

EPHESIANS 4:1 NCV

L ife is best lived on purpose. And purpose, like
everything else in the universe, begins with God.
Whether you realize it or not, God has a plan for your
life, a divine calling, a direction in which He is leading you.
When you welcome God into your heart and establish a
genuine relationship with Him, He will begin, in time, to
make His purposes known.

Sometimes, God's intentions will be clear to you; other
times, God's plan will seem uncertain at best. But even on
those difficult days when you are unsure which way to turn,
you must never lose sight of these overriding facts: God
created you for a reason; He has important work for you to
do; and He's waiting patiently for you to do it.

And the next step is up to you.

2 minutes a DAY

It is important to set goals because if you do not have
a plan, a goal, a direction, a purpose, and a focus, you are
not going to accomplish anything for the glory of God.

BILL BRIGHT

Only God's chosen task for you will ultimately satisfy.
Do not wait until it is too late to realize the privilege of
serving Him in His chosen position for you.

BETH MOORE

The Big Idea

Discovering God's purpose for your life requires a
willingness to be open. God's plan is unfolding day by day.
If you keep your eyes and your heart open, He'll reveal
His plans. God has big things in store for you, but He may
have quite a few lessons to teach you before you are fully
prepared to do His will and fulfill His purposes.

DATING & SEX

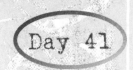

Don't Be Trapped by Envy

We can't afford to waste a minute, must not squander these precious daylight hours in frivolity and indulgence, in sleeping around and dissipation, in bickering and grabbing everything in sight. Get out of bed and get dressed! Don't loiter and linger, waiting until the very last minute. Dress yourselves in Christ, and be up and about!

ROMANS 13:13-14 MSG

B ecause we are frail, imperfect human beings, we are sometimes envious of others. But God's Word warns us that envy is sin. Thus, we must guard ourselves against the natural tendency to feel resentment and jealousy when other people experience good fortune.

As believers, we have absolutely no reason to be envious of any people on earth. After all, as Christians we are already recipients of the greatest gift in all creation: God's grace. We have been promised the gift of eternal life through God's only begotten Son, and we must count that gift as our most precious possession.

Rather than succumbing to the sin of envy, we should focus on the marvelous things that God has done for us—starting with Christ's sacrifice. And we must refrain from preoccupying ourselves with the blessings that God has chosen to give others.

2 Minutes A Day

So here's a surefire formula for a happier life (and healthier relationships): Count your own blessings and let your friends count theirs. It's the godly way to live.

more stuff to think about

When you worry about what you don't have,
you won't be able to enjoy what you do have.

CHARLES SWINDOLL

Contentment comes when we develop an attitude of gratitude for the important things we do have in our lives that we tend to take for granted if we have our eyes staring longingly at our neighbor's stuff.

DAVE RAMSEY

The Big Idea

Feelings of envy will rob you of happiness and peace. Don't allow yourself to be robbed.

DATING & SEX

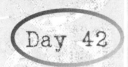

Remember That Actions Speak Louder

For the kingdom of God is not in talk but in power.
1 CORINTHIANS 4:20 HOLMAN CSB

The old saying is both familiar and true: actions speak louder than words. And as believers, we must beware: our actions should always give credence to the changes that Christ can make in the lives of those who walk with Him.

God calls upon each of us to act in accordance with His will and with respect for His commandments. If we are to be responsible believers, we must realize that it is never enough simply to hear the instructions of God; we must also live by them. And it is never enough to wait idly by while others do God's work here on earth; we, too, must act. Doing God's work is a responsibility that each of us must bear, and when we do, our loving Heavenly Father rewards our efforts with a bountiful harvest.

more stuff to think about

Every word we speak, every action we take,
has an effect on the totality of humanity.
No one can escape that privilege—or that responsibility.

LAURIE BETH JONES

It is by acts and not by ideas that people live.

HARRY EMERSON FOSDICK

Never fail to do something because you don't feel like it.
Sometimes you just have to do it now,
and you'll feel like it later.

MARIE T. FREEMAN

The Big Idea

Try as we might, we simply cannot escape the consequences
of our actions. How we behave today has a direct impact on
the rewards we will receive tomorrow. That's a lesson that
we must teach others by our words and our actions, but not
necessarily in that order.

DATING & SEX

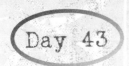

Seek Strength from God

*The LORD is my strength and my song; he has become
my victory. He is my God, and I will praise him.*

EXODUS 15:2 NLT

Where do you go to find strength? The gym? The
health food store? The espresso bar? There's
a better source of strength, of course, and that
source is God. He is a never-ending source of strength and
courage if you call upon Him.

Have you "tapped in" to the power of God? Have you
turned your life, your relationships, and your heart over to
Him—or are you muddling along under your own power?
The answer to this question will determine the quality of your
life here on earth and the destiny of your life throughout all
eternity. So start tapping in—and remember that when it
comes to strength, God is the Ultimate Source.

2 minutes A DAY

more stuff to think about

Sometimes I think spiritual and physical strength is like manna: you get just what you need for the day, no more.

SUZANNE DALE EZELL

When God is our strength, it is strength indeed; when our strength is our own, it is only weakness.

ST. AUGUSTINE

When we reach the end of our strength, wisdom, and personal resources, we enter into the beginning of his glorious provisions.

PATSY CLAIRMONT

The Big Idea

If you're energy is low or your nerves are frazzled, perhaps you need to slow down and have a heart-to-heart talk with God. And while you're at it, remember that God is bigger than your problems . . . much bigger.

DATING & SEX

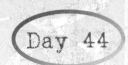

Don't Give Up on God or Yourself

*Thanks be to God! He gives us the victory through our Lord
Jesus Christ. Therefore, my dear brothers, stand firm.
Let nothing move you. Always give yourselves fully
to the work of the Lord, because you know
that your labor in the Lord is not in vain.*

1 CORINTHIANS 15:57-58 NIV

D o you sincerely want to live a life that is pleasing
to God? If so, you must remember that life is not
a sprint, it's a marathon that calls for preparation,
determination, and lots of perseverance.

Are you one of those people who doesn't give up easily,
or are you quick to bail out when the going gets tough?
If you've developed the unfortunate habit of giving up at
the first sign of trouble, it's probably time for you to have a
heart-to-heart talk with the person you see every time you
look in the mirror.

Jesus finished what He began, and so should you.
Despite His suffering, despite the shame of the cross, Jesus
was steadfast in His faithfulness to God. You, too, must
remain faithful, especially when times are tough.

Do you want to build a closer relationship with God?

Then don't give up. And if you're facing a difficult situation, remember this: whatever your problem, God can handle it. Your job is to keep persevering until He does.

more stuff to think about

Keep adding, keep walking, keep advancing; do not stop, do not turn back, do not turn from the straight road.
ST. AUGUSTINE

God never gives up on you,
so don't you ever give up on Him.
MARIE T. FREEMAN

Perseverance is more than endurance.
It is endurance combined with absolute assurance and certainty that what we are looking for is going to happen.
OSWALD CHAMBERS

The Big Idea

If things don't work out at first, don't quit. If you never try, you'll never know how good you can be.

DATING & SEX

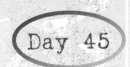

Keep Studying God's Word

Your word is a lamp to my feet and a light to my path.
PSALM 119:105 NKJV

If you want to know God, you should read the book He wrote. It's called the Bible, and it is one of the most important tools that God uses to direct your steps, to enhance your relationships, and to transform your life.

You must decide whether God's Word will be a bright spotlight that guides your path every day or a tiny nightlight that occasionally flickers in the dark. The decision to study the Bible—or not—is yours and yours alone. But make no mistake: the way that you choose to use your Bible will have a profound impact on you and your loved ones. Very profound!

more stuff to think about

I suggest you discipline yourself to spend time daily in a
systematic reading of God's Word.
Make this "quiet time" a priority that nobody can change.

WARREN WIERSBE

Walking in faith brings you to the Word of God.
There you will be healed, cleansed, fed, nurtured,
equipped, and matured.

KAY ARTHUR

The Bible is God's Word, given to us by God Himself
so we can know Him and His will for our lives.

BILLY GRAHAM

The Big Idea

Trust God's Word: Charles Swindoll writes, "There are four
words I wish we would never forget, and they are, 'God
keeps his word.'" And remember: When it comes to studying
God's Word, school is always in session.

DATING & SEX

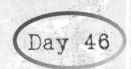

Trust the Future to God

"I say this because I know what I am planning for you,"
says the Lord. "I have good plans for you, not plans to hurt
you. I will give you hope and a good future."

JEREMIAH 29:11 NCV

How bright is your future? Well, if you're a faithful believer, God's plans for you are so bright that you'd better pack lots of sunscreen. But here's an important question: How bright do you believe your future to be? Are you expecting a terrific tomorrow, or are you dreading a terrible one? The answer you give will have a powerful impact on the way tomorrow turns out.

Do you trust in the ultimate goodness of God's plan for your life? Will you face tomorrow's challenges with optimism and hope? You should. After all, God created you for a very important reason: His reason. And you still have important work to do: His work.

Today, as you live in the present and look to the future, remember that God has an amazing plan for you. Act—and believe—accordingly.

more stuff to think about

When the train goes through a tunnel and the world becomes dark, do you jump out? Of course not. You sit still and trust the engineer to get you through.

CORRIE TEN BOOM

Contentment is trusting God even when things seem out of control.

CHARLES STANLEY

Trust in yourself and you are doomed to disappointment; trust in money and you may have it taken from you, but trust in God, and you are never to be confounded in time or eternity.

D. L. MOODY

The Big Idea

The future isn't some pie-in-the-sky dream. Hope for the future is simply one aspect of trusting God.

DATING & SEX

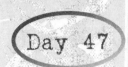

Don't Get Tired of Doing the Right Thing

Let us not become weary in doing good, for at the proper time we will reap a harvest if we do not give up.

GALATIANS 6:9 NIV

The world you live in has a way of testing your faith, your courage, and your intentions. If you intend to follow God (and if you follow through on those intentions), you'll be rewarded . . . richly rewarded. But if you cave in at the first temptation, you're headed for trouble, and fast.

So here's a foolproof formula for building better relationships and a better life: don't ever get tired of doing the right thing. When you do, you'll discover that God never gets tired of rewarding you for doing the right thing.

more stuff to think about

The life of a good religious person ought to abound
in every virtue so that he is, on the interior,
what to others he appears to be.

THOMAS À KEMPIS

Integrity is not a given factor in everyone's life.
It is a result of self-discipline, inner trust, and a decision to
be relentlessly honest in all situations in our lives.

JOHN MAXWELL

A person who gazes and keeps on gazing at Jesus becomes
like him in appearance.

E. STANLEY JONES

The Big Idea

When it comes to telling the world about your relationship
with God . . . your actions speak much more loudly than
your words . . . so behave accordingly.

DATING & SEX

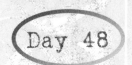

Expect His Abundance

*I have come that they may have life,
and that they may have it more abundantly.*

JOHN 10:10 NKJV

When Jesus talks of the abundant life, is He talking about material riches or earthly fame? Hardly. The Son of God came to this world, not to give it prosperity, but to give it salvation. Thankfully for Christians, our Savior's abundance is both spiritual and eternal; it never falters—even if we do—and it never dies. We need only to open our hearts to Him, and His grace becomes ours.

God's gifts are available to all, but they are not guaranteed; those gifts must be claimed by those who choose to follow Christ. As believers, we are free to accept God's gifts, or not; that choice, and the consequences that result from it, are ours and ours alone.

As we go about our daily lives, may we accept God's promise of spiritual abundance, and may we share it with a world in desperate need of the Master's healing touch.

2 minutes A DAY

more stuff to think about

If we just give God the little that we have,
we can trust Him to make it go around.

GLORIA GAITHER

If we were given all we wanted here,
our hearts would settle for this world rather than the next.

ELISABETH ELLIOT

The Son of God came to this world, not to give it prosperity,
but to give it salvation.

CRISWELL FREEMAN

The Big Idea

Abundant living may or may not include material wealth, but
abundant living always includes the spiritual riches that you
receive when you obey God's Word.

DATING & SEX

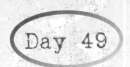

Remember That You Can Have a New Beginning

And He who sits on the throne said,
"Behold, I am making all things new."
REVELATION 21:5 NASB

Have you been involved in behaviors that have left you feeling worse about yourself, not better? If so, today is the perfect day to start putting God first in your life.

Each new day offers countless opportunities to serve God, to seek His will, and to obey His teachings. But each day also offers countless opportunities to stray from God's commandments and to wander far from His path.

Sometimes, we make a mess of things, but God has better plans of us. And, whenever we ask Him to renew our strength and guide our steps, He does so.

So if you've made mistakes in the past, and if you want to make amends, consider this day a new beginning. Consider it a fresh start, a renewed opportunity to serve your Creator with willing hands and a loving heart. Ask God to renew your sense of purpose as He guides your steps. Today is a glorious opportunity to serve God. Seize that opportunity while you can; tomorrow may indeed be too late.

more stuff to think about

Mistakes offer the possibility for redemption and a new start in God's kingdom. No matter what you're guilty of, God can restore your innocence.

BARBARA JOHNSON

Sometimes, we need a housecleaning of the heart.

CATHERINE MARSHALL

All the power of God—the same power that hung the stars in place and put the planets in their courses and transformed Earth—now resides in you to energize and strengthen you to become the person God created you to be.

ANNE GRAHAM LOTZ

The Big Idea

God is in the business of making all things new . . . including you.

DATING & SEX

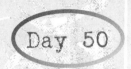

Be Patient and Trust God

Trust in him at all times, O people;
pour out your hearts to him, for God is our refuge.

PSALM 62:8 NIV

The dictionary defines the word *patience* as "the ability to be calm, tolerant, and understanding." If that describes you, you can skip the rest of this page. But, if you're like most of us, you'd better keep reading.

For most of us, patience is a hard thing to master. Why? Because we have lots of things we want (things like better relationships), and we want them NOW (if not sooner). But the Bible tells us that we must learn to wait patiently for the things that God has in store for us.

The next time you find your patience tested to the limit as you're waiting to find Mister or Miss Right, remember that the world unfolds according to God's timetable, not yours. Sometimes, you must wait patiently for God to do His work, and that's as it should be. After all, think how patient God has been with you!

2 minutes A DAY

more stuff to think about

God never hurries. There are no deadlines against
which He must work. To know this is to quiet
our spirits and relax our nerves.

A. W. TOZER

If God is slow in answering your request,
and you ask but do not promptly receive anything,
do not be upset, for you are not wiser than God.

ABRAHAM OF NATHPAR

Be patient. God is using today's difficulties to
strengthen you for tomorrow. He is equipping you.
The God who makes things grow will help you bear fruit.

MAX LUCADO

The Big Idea

Today, i will think about . . . becoming more patient with
others, with myself, and with God.

DATING & SEX

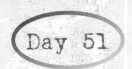

Stand Up for Your Beliefs

*Since, then, you have been raised with Christ,
set your hearts on things above, where Christ is seated
at the right hand of God. Set your minds on things above,
not on earthly things.*

COLOSSIANS 3:1-2 NIV

If you're willing to stand up for the things you believe in, you'll make better choices, and you'll build stronger relationships. But if you're one person on Sunday morning and a different person throughout the rest of the week, you'll be doing yourself—and your conscience—a big disservice.

The moment that you decide to stand up for your beliefs, you can no longer be a lukewarm, halfhearted Christian. And, when you are no longer a lukewarm Christian, God rejoices (and the devil doesn't).

So stand up for your beliefs. And remember this: in the battle of good versus evil, the devil never takes a day off . . . and neither should you.

more stuff to think about

Great tranquility has he who cares neither
for praise nor criticism.

THOMAS Á KEMPIS

It is comfortable to know that we are responsible to God
and not to man. It is a small matter to be judged
of man's judgement.

LOTTIE MOON

Don't be addicted to approval. Follow your heart.
Do what you believe God is telling you to do,
and stand firm in Him and Him alone.

JOYCE MEYER

The Big Idea

Talking about your beliefs is easy. But, making your actions
match your words is much harder. Nevertheless, if you really
want to be honest with yourself, then you must make your
actions match your beliefs. Period.

DATING & SEX

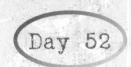

Do the Right Thing

*Knowing what is right is like deep water in the heart;
a wise person draws from the well within.*
PROVERBS 20:5 MSG

If you want to know God, you should obey God. But obeying Him isn't always easy. You live in a world that presents countless temptations to stray far from God's path. So here's some timely advice: when you're confronted with sin, walk—or better yet run—in the opposite direction.

When you seek righteousness for yourself—and when you seek the companionship of people who do likewise—you will reap the spiritual rewards that God has in store for you. When you live in accordance with God's commandments, you will be blessed. When you genuinely seek to follow in the footsteps of God's Son, you will experience God's presence, God's peace, and God's abundance.

So make yourself this promise: Support only those activities that further God's kingdom and your own spiritual growth. Then, prepare to reap the blessings that God has promised to all those who live according to His will and His Word.

more stuff to think about

Many people never receive God's best for them because they are addicted to the approval of others.

JOYCE MEYER

What you do reveals what you believe about God, regardless of what you say. When God reveals what He has purposed to do, you face a crisis—a decision time. God and the world can tell from your response what you really believe about God.

HENRY BLACKABY

Discrepancies between values and practices create chaos in a person's life.

JOHN MAXWELL

The Big Idea

When it comes to doing the right thing, don't put it off. If you're not willing to do the right thing today, why should you (or anybody else, for that matter) expect you to change tomorrow?

DATING & SEX

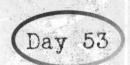

Don't Let Your Problems Get You Down

People who do what is right may have many problems,
but the Lord will solve them all.

PSALM 34:19 NCV

All of us face those occasional days when the traffic jams and the dog gobbles up the homework. But, when we find ourselves overtaken by the frustrations of life, we must catch ourselves, take a deep breath, and lift our thoughts upward.

Although we must occasionally struggle to rise above the distractions and disappointments of tough times (or tough relationships), we need never struggle alone. God is here—eternally and faithfully, with infinite patience and love. And our friends and family members are also willing to help us restore perspective and peace to our souls. Our job is to let them.

2 minutes A DAY

more stuff to think about

Keep your feet on the ground, but let your heart soar
as high as it will. Refuse to be average or to surrender
to the chill of your spiritual environment.

A. W. TOZER

Hope looks for the good in people, opens doors for people,
discovers what can be done to help, lights a candle,
does not yield to cynicism. Hope sets people free.

BARBARA JOHNSON

The Big Idea

Be a realistic optimist: Your attitude toward the future will
help create your future. So think realistically about yourself
and your situation while making a conscious effort to focus
on hopes, not fears. When you do, you'll put the self-
fulfilling prophecy to work for you.

DATING & SEX

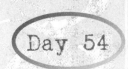

Looking Good?

He said to them, "You make yourselves look good in front of people, but God knows what is really in your hearts. What is important to people is hateful in God's sight."

Luke 16:15 NCV

You live in a society that is obsessed with "looking good." Everywhere you turn, you're confronted with a steady stream of subtle messages that try to convince you it's more important to look good than to be good. These messages are not only false, but they are also dangerous to your spiritual and emotional health.

Would you like to build a better life and stronger relationships? If so, here's a great place to start: worry less about appearances and more about substance. When you do, you may find that you're a little out of step with the world, which is perfectly okay. After all, the world sees people and things as they appear to be, but God sees them as they really are . . . and that's the way you should try to see them, too.

more stuff to think about

The temptation of the age is to look good
without being good.

BRENNAN MANNING

You will quickly be deceived if you look only to the outward
appearance of men, and you will often be disappointed
if you seek comfort and gain in them.

THOMAS À KEMPIS

You can't judge a book by its cover.

OLD-TIME SAYING

The Big Idea

Appearances, appearances, appearances: Don't be too
worried about what you look like on the outside; be more
concerned about the kind of person you are on the inside.
God loves you just like you are . . . and now, it's your turn to
do the same thing.

DATING & SEX

Learn to Communicate

Rash language cuts and maims,
but there is healing in the words of the wise.
PROVERBS 12:18 MSG

If you want to build strong relationships, you should teach yourself to become an effective communicator. And that's exactly what God wants you to do. God's Word reminds us that "Reckless words pierce like a sword, but the tongue of the wise brings healing" (Proverbs 12:18 NIV).

Today, make this promise to yourself: vow to be an honest, effective, encouraging communicator at school, at home, at church, and everyplace in between. Speak wisely, not impulsively. Use words of kindness and praise, not words of anger or derision. Learn how to be truthful without being cruel. Remember that you have the power to heal others or to injure them, to lift others up or to hold them back. And when you learn how to lift them up, you'll soon discover that you've lifted yourself up, too.

2 minutes A DAY

more stuff to think about

Happy the man whose words issue from
the Holy Spirit and not from himself.

ANTHONY OF PADUA

Like dynamite, God's power is only latent power
until it is released. You can release God's dynamite power
into people's lives and the world through faith,
your words, and prayer.

BILL BRIGHT

Attitude and the spirit in which we communicate
are as important as the words we say.

CHARLES STANLEY

The Big Idea

Think First, Speak Second: If you blurt out the first thing that
comes into your head, you may say things that are better left
unsaid.

DATING & SEX

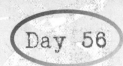

Don't Hang Out with Cruel People

My dear friend, do not follow what is bad;
follow what is good.
3 JOHN 1:11 NCV

Face it: sometimes people can be very cruel. And when people are unkind to you or to your friends, you may be tempted to strike back in anger. Don't do it! Instead, remember that God corrects other people's behaviors in His own way, and He doesn't need your help. And remember that God has commanded you to forgive others, just as you, too, must sometimes seek forgiveness from them.

So, when other people are cruel, as they most certainly will be from time to time, what should you do? 1. Politely speak up for yourself (and for people who can't speak up for themselves); 2. Forgive everybody as quickly as you can; 3. Leave the rest up to God, and 4. Move on with your life by making sure that you don't consistently hang out with cruel people.

2 minutes A DAY

more stuff to think about

Pride opens the door to every other sin, for once we are more concerned with our reputation than our character, there is no end to the things we will do just to make ourselves "look good" before others.

WARREN WIERSBE

Sour godliness is the devil's religion.

JOHN WESLEY

Nothing can be more dangerous than keeping wicked companions. They communicate the infection of their vices to all who associate with them.

ST. JEAN BAPTISTE DE LA SALLE

The Big Idea

A thoughtful Christian doesn't follow the crowd . . . a thoughtful Christian follows Jesus.

Worship Every Day

Worship the Lord your God and . . . serve Him only.
MATTHEW 4:10 HOLMAN CSB

If you really want to enjoy a better life (and better relationships), here's something you can do: try worshipping God seven days a week, not just on Sundays.

God has a wonderful plan for your life, and an important part of that plan includes the time that you set aside for praise and worship. Every life, including yours, is based upon some form of worship. The question is not whether you will worship, but what you worship.

If you choose to worship God, you will receive a bountiful harvest of joy, peace, and abundance. But if you distance yourself from God by foolishly worshiping earthly possessions and personal gratification, you're making a huge mistake. So do yourself a favor: Worship God today and every day. Worship Him with sincerity and thanksgiving. Write His name on your heart and rest assured that He, too, has written your name on His.

2 minutes A DAY

more stuff to think about

We are never more fulfilled than when our longing for God is met by His presence in our lives.

BILLY GRAHAM

Each time, before you intercede, be quiet first and worship God in His glory. Think of what He can do and how He delights to hear the prayers of His redeemed people. Think of your place and privilege in Christ, and expect great things!

ANDREW MURRAY

The Big Idea

Worship is not meant to be boxed up in a church building on Sunday morning. To the contrary, praise and worship should be woven into the very fabric of your life. Do you take time each day to worship your Father in heaven, or do you wait until Sunday morning to praise Him for His blessings? The answer to this question will, in large part, determine the quality and direction of your life. So worship accordingly.

DATING & SEX

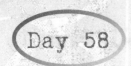

Let God Guide the Way

The true children of God are those who let God's Spirit lead them.
ROMANS 8:14 NCV

The Bible promises that God will guide you if you let Him. Your job is to let Him. But sometimes, you will be tempted to do otherwise. Sometimes, you'll be tempted to go along with the crowd; other times, you'll be tempted to do things your way, not God's way. When you feel these temptations, resist them.

God has promised that when you ask for His help, He will not withhold it. So ask. Ask Him to meet the needs of your day. Ask Him to lead you, to protect you, and to correct you. And trust the answers He gives.

God stands at the door and waits. When you knock, He opens. When you ask, He answers. Your task, of course, is to seek His guidance prayerfully, confidently, and often.

more stuff to think about

If we want to hear God's voice, we must surrender
our minds and hearts to Him.

BILLY GRAHAM

Are you serious about wanting God's guidance to become
a personal reality in your life? The first step is to
tell God that you know you can't manage your own life;
that you need his help.

CATHERINE MARSHALL

We have ample evidence that the Lord is able to guide.
The promises cover every imaginable situation.
All we need to do is to take the hand he stretches out.

ELISABETH ELLIOT

The Big Idea

Pray for guidance. When you seek it, He will give it.
(Luke 11:9)

DATING & SEX

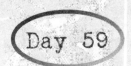

Pay Attention to What's Happening Around You

*Pay careful attention, then, to how you walk—
not as unwise people but as wise.*
EPHESIANS 5:15 HOLMAN CSB

You can learn a lot about life, love, and the pursuit of happiness by paying attention to the things that happen around you—so keep your eyes and ears open. And while you're at it, please try to remember that "denial" isn't a big river in Egypt (it is, in truth, the natural human tendency to ignore little problems until they grow too big to ignore).

God is trying to teach you things, and you can learn these lessons the easy way (by paying attention, by learning from other people's mistakes, and by obeying God's commandments) or the hard way (by making your own mistakes, and by continuing to make them over and over again until you finally learn something). Of course, it's better to learn things sooner rather than later . . . starting now. So what are you waiting for?

2 minutes A DAY

more stuff to think about

Experience has taught me that the Shepherd is far more willing to show His sheep the path than the sheep are to follow. He is endlessly merciful, patient, tender, and loving. If we, His stupid and wayward sheep, really want to be led, we will without fail be led. Of that I am sure.

ELISABETH ELLIOT

Believe and do what God says. The life-changing consequences will be limitless, and the results will be confidence and peace of mind.

FRANKLIN GRAHAM

Much guilt arises in the life of the believer from practicing the chameleon life of environmental adaptation.

BETH MOORE

The Big Idea

Do you find yourself in the same kind of trouble over and over again? If so, there's something in your life that needs to be fixed—and you've probably been trying to ignore it. Ignore no more! You'll never fix the problems that you're unwilling to acknowledge.

DATING & SEX

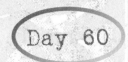

Remember
the Golden Rule

Do to others what you want them to do to you.
Matthew 7:12 NCV

Life is simply better when we treat other people in the same way we would want to be treated if we were in their shoes. Things go better when we're courteous and compassionate. Graciousness, humility, and kindness are all virtues we should strive for. But sometimes, we fall short. Sometimes, amid the busyness and confusion of everyday life, we may neglect to share a kind word or a kind deed. This oversight hurts others, and it hurts us as well.

Today, slow yourself down and be alert for those who need your smile, your kind words, your hug, or your helping hand. Make kindness a centerpiece of your dealings with others. They will be blessed, and you will be, too. But not necessarily in that order.

more stuff to think about

We should behave to our friends as we would wish
our friends to behave to us.

ARISTOTLE

The Golden Rule starts at home,
but it should never stop there.

MARIE T. FREEMAN

It is wrong for anyone to be anxious to receive more from
his neighbor than he himself is willing to give to God.

ST. FRANCIS OF ASSISI

The Big Idea

How would you feel? When you're trying to decide how to
treat another person, ask yourself this question: "How would
I feel if somebody treated me that way?" Then, treat the
other person the way that you would want to be treated.

DATING & SEX

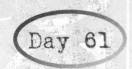

Remember Christ's Love

*For I am persuaded that neither death nor life,
nor angels nor principalities nor powers, nor things present
nor things to come, nor height nor depth, nor any other
created thing, shall be able to separate us from the love of
God which is in Christ Jesus our Lord.*

ROMANS 8:38-39 NKJV

How much does Christ love us? More than we, as mere mortals, can comprehend. His love is perfect and steadfast. Even though we are imperfect and wayward, the Good Shepherd cares for us still. Even though we have fallen far short of the Father's commandments, Christ loves us with a power and depth that are beyond our understanding. The sacrifice that Jesus made upon the cross was made for each of us, and His love endures to the edge of eternity and beyond.

Christ's love changes everything, including your relationships. When you accept His gift of grace, you are transformed, not only for today, but also for all eternity.

Jesus is waiting patiently for you to invite Him into your heart. Please don't make Him wait a single minute longer.

more stuff to think about

We are of such value to God that He came to live among
us . . . and to guide us home. He will go to any length to
seek us, even to being lifted high upon the cross
to draw us back to Himself. We can only respond
by loving God for His love.

CATHERINE OF SIENA

God expressed His love in sending the Holy Spirit
to live within us.

CHARLES STANLEY

God is my heavenly Father. He loves me with
an everlasting love. The proof of that is the Cross.

ELISABETH ELLIOT

The Big Idea

Jesus loves you . . . His love is amazing, it's wonderful, and
it's meant for you.

DATING & SEX

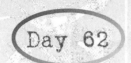

Remember the Importance of Courtesy

Be hospitable to one another without grumbling.
1 PETER 4:9 NKJV

Did Christ instruct us in matters of etiquette and courtesy? Of course He did. Christ's instructions are clear: "In everything, therefore, treat people the same way you want them to treat you, for this is the Law and the Prophets" (Matthew 7:12 NASB). Jesus did not say, "In some things, treat people as you wish to be treated." And, He did not say, "From time to time, treat others with kindness." Christ said that we should treat others as we wish to be treated in every aspect of our daily lives. This, of course, is a tall order indeed, but as Christians, we are commanded to do our best.

Today, be a little kinder than necessary to family members, friends, and total strangers. And, as you consider all the things that Christ has done in your life, honor Him with your words and with your deeds. He expects no less, and He deserves no less.

2 minutes A DAY

When you extend hospitality to others,
you're not trying to impress people;
you're trying to reflect God to them.

MAX LUCADO

Only the courteous can love,
but it is love that makes them courteous.

C. S. LEWIS

Courtesy is contagious.

MARIE T. FREEMAN

The Big Idea

Remember: courtesy isn't optional. If you disagree, do
so without being disagreeable; if you're angry, hold your
tongue; if you're frustrated or tired, don't argue . . . take a
nap.

DATING & SEX

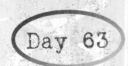

Remember That Your Circumstances Change but God Does Not

The LORD is my rock, my fortress and my savior; my God is my rock in whom I find protection. He is my shield, the strength of my salvation, and my stronghold.

PSALM 18:2 NLT

We live in a world that is always changing, but we worship a God that never changes—thank goodness! That means that we can be comforted in the knowledge that our Heavenly Father is the rock that simply cannot be moved: "I am the LORD, I do not change" (Malachi 3:6 NKJV).

The next time you face difficult circumstances, tough times, unfair treatment, or a broken relationship, remember that some things never change—things like the love that you feel in your heart for your family and friends . . . and the love that God feels for you. So, instead of worrying too much about life's inevitable challenges, focus your energies on finding solutions. Have faith in your own abilities, do your best to solve your problems, and leave the rest up to God.

2 minutes A DAY

more stuff to think about

The God who spoke still speaks. He comes into our world. He comes into your world. He comes to do what you can't.

MAX LUCADO

His descent to our lowliness is the supreme expression of his power.

ST. GREGORY OF NYSSA

God does not give us everything we want, but He does fulfill all His promises as He leads us along the best and straightest paths to Himself.

DIETRICH BONHOEFFER

The Big Idea

Change is inevitable . . . you can either roll with it or be rolled over by it. Choose the former.

DATING & SEX

Don't Be Too Critical

Do not judge, and you will not be judged.
Do not condemn, and you will not be condemned.
LUKE 6:37 NIV

From experience, we know that it is easier to criticize than to correct; we understand that it is easier to find faults than solutions; and we realize that excessive criticism is usually destructive, not productive. Yet the urge to criticize others remains a powerful temptation for most of us. Our task, as obedient believers, is to break the twin habits of negative thinking and critical speech.

Negativity is highly contagious: we give it to others who, in turn, give it back to us. This cycle can be broken by positive thoughts, heartfelt prayers, and encouraging words. As thoughtful servants of a loving God, we can use the transforming power of Christ's love to break the chains of negativity. And we should.

2 minutes A DAY

more stuff to think about

What difference does it make to you what someone else becomes, or says, or does? You do not need to answer for others, only for yourself.

THOMAS À KEMPIS

If I long to improve my brother, the first step toward doing so is to improve myself.

CHRISTINA ROSSETTI

The scrutiny we give other people should be for ourselves.

OSWALD CHAMBERS

The Big Idea

If you're tempted to be critical of others, remember that your ability to judge others requires a level of insight that you simply don't have. So do everybody (including yourself) a favor: don't criticize.

DATING & SEX

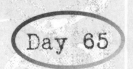

Day 65

Learn to Say No

Discretion will protect you and understanding will guard you.
PROVERBS 2:11 NIV

When your peers encourage you to do things that you know are wrong, do you have enough confidence to say no? Hopefully so. But if you haven't quite learned the art of saying no, don't feel like the Lone Ranger—plenty of people much older than you still have trouble standing up for themselves.

An important part of growing up is learning how to assert yourself. Another part of growing up is learning when to say no. For most people, these are lessons that take a long time to learn, so if you're wise, you'll start learning them sooner rather than later. Remember: you have the right to say no, and you have the right to say it right now!

2 MINUTES A DAY

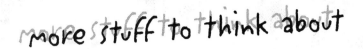

more stuff to think about

Choose the opposition of the whole world
rather than offend Jesus.

THOMAS À KEMPIS

A thoughtful Christian doesn't follow the crowd unless the
crowd is following Jesus.

ANONYMOUS

For better or worse, you will eventually become more
and more like the people you associate with. So why not
associate with people who make you better, not worse?

MARIE T. FREEMAN

The Big Idea

Slow down! If you're about to make an important decision,
don't be impulsive. Remember: big decisions have
big consequences, and if you don't think about those
consequences now, you may pay a big price later.

DATING & SEX

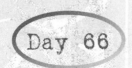

Live Triumphantly

The lines of purpose in your lives never grow slack, tightly tied as they are to your future in heaven, kept taut by hope.
COLOSSIANS 1:5 MSG

Are you living the triumphant life that God has promised? Or are you, instead, a spiritual shrinking violet? As you ponder that question, consider this: God does not intend that you live a life that is commonplace or mediocre. And He doesn't want you to hide your light "under a basket." Instead, He wants you to "Let your light so shine before men, that they may see your good works and glorify your Father in heaven" (Matthew 5:16 NKJV). In short, God wants you to live a triumphant life so that others might know precisely what it means to be a believer.

The Christian life should be a triumphal celebration, a daily exercise in thanksgiving and praise. Join that celebration today. And while you're at it, make sure that you let everybody—friends, family members, and dates—know that you've joined.

2 minutes A DAY

more stuff to think about

Continually restate to yourself what the purpose
of your life is.

OSWALD CHAMBERS

To do good things in the world, first you must know who you
are and what gives meaning to your life.

PAULA BROWNLEE

Four prerequisites needed to find your gift are being
a Christian, believing in spiritual gifts,
being willing to work, and praying.

PETER WAGNER

The Big Idea

God still has a wonderful plan for your life. And the time to
start looking for that plan—and living it—is now.
(Psalm 16:11)

DATING & SEX

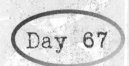

Stay Humble!

Humble yourselves, therefore, under God's mighty hand,
that he may lift you up in due time.
1 PETER 5:6 NIV

On the road to spiritual and personal growth, pride is a massive roadblock. Simply put, the more prideful you are, the more difficult it is to know God.

When you experience success, it's easy to puff out your chest and proclaim, "I did that!" But it's wrong. Dietrich Bonhoeffer was correct when he observed, "It is very easy to overestimate the importance of our own achievements in comparison with what we owe others." In other words, reality breeds humility.

So if you want to know God better—and if you want to be successful in life and love—be humble. Otherwise, you'll be building a roadblock between you and your Creator (and that's a very bad thing to do!).

2 minutes a day

more stuff to think about

Nothing sets a person so much out of
the devil's reach as humility.

JONATHAN EDWARDS

I can usually sense that a leading is from the Holy Spirit
when it calls me to humble myself, to serve somebody, to
encourage somebody, or to give something away. Very rarely
will the evil one lead us to do those kind of things.

BILL HYBELS

Do you wish to rise? Begin by descending.
You plan a tower that will pierce the clouds?
Lay first the foundation of humility.

ST. AUGUSTINE

The Big Idea

Do you value humility above status? If so, God will smile
upon your endeavors. But if you value status above humility,
you're inviting God's displease. In short, humility pleases
God; pride does not.

DATING & SEX

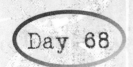

Understand
the Importance
of Encouragement

Pleasant words are like a honeycomb,
Sweetness to the soul and health to the bones.
PROVERBS 16:24 NKJV

Life is a team sport, and all of us need occasional pats on the back from our teammates. As Christians, we are called upon to spread the Good News of Christ, and we are also called to spread a message of encouragement and hope to the world.

Whether you realize it or not, many people with whom you come in contact every day are in desperate need of a smile or an encouraging word. The world can be a difficult place, and countless friends and family members may be troubled by the challenges of everyday life. Since you don't always know who needs your help, the best strategy is to try to encourage all the people who cross your path. So today, be a world-class source of encouragement to everyone you meet. Never has the need been greater.

2 MINUTES A DAY

more stuff to think about

We can never untangle all the woes in other people's lives.
We can't produce miracles overnight.
But we can bring a cup of cool water to a thirsty soul,
or a scoop of laughter to a lonely heart.

BARBARA JOHNSON

How many people stop because so few say, "Go!"

CHARLES SWINDOLL

I'd rather see a sermon than hear one any day;
I'd rather one should walk with me than merely tell the way.

EDGAR A. GUEST

The Big Idea

Sometimes, even very few words can make a very big difference. As Fanny Crosby observed, "A single word, if spoken in a friendly spirit, may be sufficient to turn one from dangerous error."

DATING & SEX

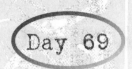

Enthusiasm for Life

Celebrate God all day, every day. I mean, revel in him!
PHILIPPIANS 4:4 MSG

A re you "burning" with enthusiasm about your life, your friends, your relationships, and your future? If so, congratulations, and keep up the good work! But, if your spiritual batteries are running low, perhaps you're spending too much energy focusing on your losses and too little time planning for future victories.

Writer Sara Jordan has this simple (but effective) advice: "Every day give yourself a good mental shampoo."

So if you're feeling tired or troubled, or both, don't despair. Instead, take time to count your blessings as you focus on things positive. And while you're at it, seek strength from the Source that never fails. When you sincerely petition God, He will give you all the strength you need to live victoriously through Him.

more stuff to think about

There seems to be a chilling fear of holy enthusiasm among the people of God. We try to tell how happy we are— but we remain so well-controlled that there are very few waves of glory experienced in our midst.

A. W. TOZER

Consider every day a new beginning, and always act with the same fervour as on the first day you began.

ANTHONY OF PADUA

One of the great needs in the church today is for every Christian to become enthusiastic about his faith in Jesus Christ.

BILLY GRAHAM

The Big Idea

If you become excited about life . . . life will become an exciting adventure.

DATING & SEX

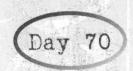

Don't Indulge in Gossip

A useless person causes trouble,
and a gossip ruins friendships.
Proverbs 16:28 NCV

Face it: gossip is bad—and the Bible clearly tells us that gossip is wrong.

When we say things that we don't want other people to know we said, we're being somewhat dishonest, but if the things we say aren't true, we're being very dishonest. Either way, we have done something that we may regret later, especially when the other person finds out.

So do yourself a big favor: don't gossip. It's a waste of words, and it's the wrong thing to do. You'll feel better about yourself if you don't gossip (and other people will feel better about you, too). So don't do it!

more stuff to think about

Those who, to please their listeners, avoid giving a forthright declaration of the will of God become slaves of those they would please and abandon the service of God.

ST. BASIL THE GREAT

We are in a continual battle with the spiritual forces of evil, but we will triumph when we yield to God's leading and call on His powerful presence in prayer.

SHIRLEY DOBSON

The battle of the tongue is won not in the mouth, but in the heart.

ANNIE CHAPMAN

The Big Idea

Watch what you say. Don't say something behind someone's back that you wouldn't say to that person directly.

DATING & SEX

Integrity Matters

A good name is more desirable than great riches;
to be esteemed is better than silver or gold.
PROVERBS 22:1 NIV

Hey, would you like a time-tested, ironclad formula for successful relationships? Here it is: guard your integrity like you guard your wallet.

It has been said on many occasions and in many ways that honesty is the best policy. For Christians, it is far more important to note that honesty is God's policy. And if we are to be servants worthy of our Savior, Jesus Christ, we must be honest, forthright, and trustworthy.

Telling the truth means telling the whole truth. And that means summoning the courage to deliver bad news when necessary. And for some of us, especially those of us who are card-carrying people pleasers, telling the whole truth can be difficult indeed (especially if we're pretty sure that the truth will make somebody mad). Still, if we wish to fashion successful lives, we've got to learn to be totally truthful—part-time truth-telling doesn't cut the mustard.

Sometimes, honesty is difficult; sometimes, honesty is painful; sometimes, honesty is inconvenient; but honesty is always God's way. In the Book of Proverbs, we read,

"The Lord detests lying lips, but he delights in men who are truthful" (12:22 NIV). Clearly, truth is God's way, and it must be our way, too, even when telling the truth is difficult.

Integrity is a sign of maturity.

CHARLES SWINDOLL

There's nothing like the power of integrity.
It is a characteristic so radiant, so steady,
so consistnet, so beautiful, that it makes
a permanent picture in our minds.

FRANKLIN GRAHAM

We can talk about faith, but what we live shows
the true faith behind the words.

JAY KESLER

The Big Idea

Today, think about ways you can remove yourself from situations that might compromise your integrity.

DATING & SEX

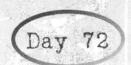

Take Your Concerns to God

Cast your burden upon the LORD and He will sustain you:
He will never allow the righteous to be shaken.
PSALM 55:22 NASB

The Bible promises this: tough times are temporary but God's love is not—God's love endures forever. So what does that mean to you? Just this: From time to time, everybody faces disappointments and broken relationships—so will you. And when tough times arrive, God always stands ready to protect you and to heal you. Your task is straightforward: you must share your burdens with Him.

As Corrie ten Boom observed, "Any concern that is too small to be turned into a prayer is too small to be made into a burden." Those are comforting words, especially during difficult days.

Whatever the size of your challenges, God is big enough to handle them. Ask for His help today, with faith and with fervor. Instead of turning things over in your mind, turn them over to God in prayer. Instead of worrying about your next decision, ask God to lead the way. Cast your burdens upon the One who cannot be shaken, and rest assured that He always hears your prayers.

more stuff to think about

Claim all of God's promises in the Bible. Your sins,
your worries, your life—you may cast them all on Him.

CORRIE TEN BOOM

Our fears for today, our worries about tomorrow,
and even the powers of hell can't keep God's love away.

BILL BRIGHT

Anxiety does not empty tomorrow of its sorrows,
but it empties today of its strength.

C. H. SPURGEON

The Big Idea

Controllable Worries About Uncontrollable Problems:
Assiduously divide your areas of concern into two categories:
those you can control and those you cannot. Resolve never
to waste time or energy worrying about the latter.

DATING & SEX

Make God the Cornerstone

*For the eyes of the Lord are on the righteous
and his ears are attentive to their prayer,
but the Lord is against those who do evil.*

1 Peter 3:12 NIV

Have you made God the cornerstone of your life and your relationships, or is He relegated to a few hours on Sunday morning? Have you genuinely allowed God to reign over every corner of your heart, or have you attempted to place Him in a spiritual compartment? The answer to these questions will determine the direction of your day and your life.

God loves you. In times of trouble, He will comfort you; in times of sorrow, He will dry your tears. When you are weak or sorrowful, God is as near as your next breath. He stands at the door of your heart and waits. Welcome Him in and allow Him to rule. And then, accept the peace and the strength and the protection, and the abundance that only God can give.

2 minutes A DAY

more stuff to think about

I have so much to do that I shall spend
the first three hours of the day in prayer.

MARTIN LUTHER

God is everything. My focus must be on him,
seeking to know him more completely and allowing him
full possession of my life.

MARY MORRISON SUGGS

Prayer does not fit us for the greater work;
prayer is the greater work.

OSWALD CHAMBERS

The Big Idea

Finding time for God takes time . . . and it's up to you to
find it. The world is constantly vying for your attention, and
sometimes the noise can be deafening. Remember the words
of Elisabeth Elliot; she said, "The world is full of noise. Let us
learn the art of silence, stillness, and solitude."

DATING & SEX

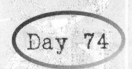

Day 74

Paying Attention to God

Your heart will be where your treasure is.
LUKE 12:34 NCV

Jesus deserves your undivided attention. Are you giving it to Him? Hopefully so.

When you focus your thoughts and prayers on the One from Galilee, you'll start building a better life and better relationships. But beware: the world will try to convince you that "other things" are more important than your faith. These messages are both false and dangerous—don't believe them.

When it comes to your spiritual, emotional, and personal growth, absolutely nothing is more important than your faith. So do yourself and your loved ones a favor: focus on God and His only begotten Son. Your loved ones will be glad you did . . . and so will you.

2 minutes a day

more stuff to think about

He doesn't need an abundance of words.
He doesn't need a dissertation about your life.
He just wants your attention. He wants your heart.

KATHY TROCCOLI

Make a plan now to keep a daily appointment with God.
The enemy is going to tell you to set it aside, but you must
carve out the time. If you're too busy to meet with the Lord,
friend, then you are simply too busy.

CHARLES SWINDOLL

If we really believe not only that God exists but also that
God is actively present in our lives—healing, teaching, and
guiding—we need to set aside a time and space
to give God our undivided attention.

HENRI NOUWEN

The Big Idea

The world wants you to focus on "stuff." God wants you to
focus on His Son. Trust God.

DATING & SEX

Share Your Faith

*And I say to you, anyone who acknowledges Me before men,
the Son of Man will also acknowledge him before the angels
of God; but whoever denies Me before men will be denied
before the angels of God.*

LUKE 12:8-9 HOLMAN CSB

Genuine faith was never meant to be locked up in the heart of a believer—to the contrary, it is meant to be shared with the world. But, if you sincerely wish to share your faith, you must first find it.

How can you find and strengthen your faith? Through praise, through worship, through fellowship, through Bible study, and through prayer. When you do these things, your faith will become stronger, and you will find ways to share your beliefs with your family, with your friends, with your dates, and with the world. And when you do, everybody wins.

2 minutes A DAY

more stuff to think about

To take up the cross means that you take your stand for the Lord Jesus no matter what it costs.

BILLY GRAHAM

Usually it is those who know Him that bring Him to others. That is why the Church, the whole body of Christians showing Him to one another, is so important.

C. S. LEWIS

Our Lord is searching for people who will make a difference. Christians dare not dissolve into the background or blend into the neutral scenery of the world.

CHARLES SWINDOLL

The Big Idea

If your eternity with God is secure (because you believe in Jesus), you have a profound responsibility to tell as many people as you can about the eternal life that Christ offers to those who believe in Him.

DATING & SEX

Nurture Your Relationship with God

Be silent before the LORD and wait expectantly for Him.

PSALM 37:7 HOLMAN CSB

Are you willing to place God first in your life? And, are you willing to welcome God's Son into your heart? Unless you can honestly answer these questions with a resounding yes, then your relationship with God isn't what it could be or should be.

As you think about the nature of your relationship with God, remember this: you will always have some type of relationship with Him—it is inevitable that your life must be lived in relationship to God. The question is not if you will have a relationship with Him; the burning question is whether or not that relationship will be one that seeks to honor Him.

Thankfully, God is always available, He's always ready to forgive, and He's waiting to hear from you now. The rest, of course, is up to you.

more stuff to think about

Life is not a journey you want to make on autopilot.

PAULA RINEHART

If you, too, will learn to wait upon God, to get alone with
Him, and remain silent so that you can hear His voice when
He is ready to speak to you, what a difference it
will make in your life!

KAY ARTHUR

Speed-reading may be a good thing, but it was never meant
for the Bible. It takes calm, thoughtful, prayerful meditation
on the Word to extract its deepest nourishment.

VANCE HAVNER

The Big Idea

Do you try to spend quiet moments with God every day of
the week? If so, keep it up. If not, why not?

DATING & SEX

Remember That Sin Enslaves

Jesus responded, "I assure you:
Everyone who commits sin is a slave of sin."
JOHN 8:34 HOLMAN CSB

B ecause we are creatures of free will, we may disobey God whenever we choose. But when we do so, we put ourselves and our loved ones in peril. Why? Because disobedience invites disaster. We cannot sin against God without consequences. We cannot live outside His will without injury. We cannot distance ourselves from God without hardening our hearts. We cannot yield to the ever-tempting distractions of our world and, at the same time, enjoy God's peace.

Sometimes, in a futile attempt to justify our behaviors, we make a distinction between "big" sins and "little" ones. To do so is a mistake of "big" proportions. Sins of all shapes and sizes have the power to do us great harm. And in a world where sin is big business, that's certainly a sobering thought.

more stuff to think about

Before we can be filled with the Living Water, we must be cleansed of sin. Before we can be cleansed of sin, we must be convicted. And sometimes it's painful. And shameful.

ANNE GRAHAM LOTZ

We cannot out-sin God's ability to forgive us.

BETH MOORE

He loved us even while we were yet sinners at war with Him!

BILL BRIGHT

The Big Idea

Sometimes immorality is obvious and sometimes it's not. So beware: the most subtle forms of sin are often the most dangerous.

DATING & SEX

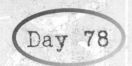

Be Still

Be still, and know that I am God.
PSALM 46:10 NKJV

The Bible teaches that a wonderful way to get to know God is simply to be still and listen to Him. But sometimes, you may find it hard to slow down and listen.

As the demands of everyday life weigh down upon you, you may be tempted to ignore God's presence or—worse yet—to rebel against His commandments. But, when you quiet yourself and acknowledge His presence, God touches your heart, restores your spirits, and gives you the perspective you need to make good decisions. So why not let Him do it right now? If you really want to get to know your Heavenly Father, silence is a wonderful place to start.

2 minutes A DAY

more stuff to think about

Instead of waiting for the feeling, wait upon God.
You can do this by growing still and quiet, then expressing in
prayer what your mind knows is true about Him,
even if your heart doesn't feel it at this moment.

SHIRLEY DOBSON

Silence is a gift of God, to let us speak
more intimately with Him.

VINCENT PALLOTTI

Deepest communion with God is beyond words,
on the other side of silence.

MADELEINE L'ENGLE

The Big Idea

Want to talk to God? Then don't make Him shout.
If you really want to hear from God, go to a quiet place
and listen. If you keep listening long enough and carefully
enough, He'll start talking.

DATING & SEX

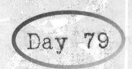

Take Time to Praise Him!

I will praise You with my whole heart.
PSALM 138:1 NKJV

If you're like most folks on the planet, you're a very busy person. Your life is probably hectic, demanding, and complicated. And when the demands of life leave you rushing from place to place with scarcely a moment to spare, you may not take time to praise your Creator. Big mistake.

The Bible makes it clear: it pays to praise God. Worship and praise should be a part of everything you do. Otherwise, you quickly lose perspective as you fall prey to the demands of everyday life.

Do you sincerely desire to know God in a more meaningful way? Then praise Him for who He is and for what He has done for you. And please don't wait until Sunday morning—praise Him all day long, every day, for as long as you live . . . and then for all eternity.

2 minutes A DAY

more stuff to think about

The Creator loves you very much since He gives you so many good things. Therefore, be careful not to be ungrateful, but strive always to praise God.

ST. FRANCIS OF ASSISI

Praising God is one of the highest and purest acts of religion. In prayer we act like men; in praise we act like angels.

THOMAS WATSON

All our life is like a day of celebration for us; we are convinced, in fact, that God is always everywhere. We work while singing; we sail while reciting hymns; we accomplish all other occupations of life while praying.

CLEMENT OF ALEXANDRIA

The Big Idea

Praise Him! One of the big reasons you should attend church is to praise God. But, you need not wait until Sunday rolls around to thank your Heavenly Father. Instead, you can praise Him many times each day by saying silent prayers that only He can hear.

DATING & SEX

Choose Wise Role Models

Spend time with the wise and you will become wise.
PROVERBS 13:20 NCV

Here's a simple yet effective way to strengthen your faith and your relationships: Choose role models whose faith in God is strong.

When you emulate godly people, you become a more godly person yourself. That's why you should seek out mentors who, by their words and their presence, make you a better person and a better Christian.

Today, as a gift to yourself, select, from your friends and family members, a mentor whose judgment you trust. Then listen carefully to your mentor's advice and be willing to accept that advice, even if accepting it requires effort or pain, or both. Consider your mentor to be God's gift to you. Thank God for that gift, and use it for the glory of His kingdom.

more stuff to think about

God often keeps us on the path by guiding us through
the counsel of friends and trusted spiritual advisors.

BILL HYBELS

Do not open your heart to every man, but discuss your
affairs with one who is wise and who fears God.

THOMAS À KEMPIS

The effective mentor strives to help a man or woman
discover what they can be in Christ and then holds them
accountable to become that person.

HOWARD HENDRICKS

The Big Idea

Talk to the experts: Your mentors may not have all of the
answers, but at least they'll know most of the questions! So
ask, listen, and learn.

DATING & SEX

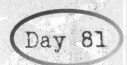

Stand Up Against the Media's Messages

My dear friends, don't let public opinion influence how you live out our glorious, Christ-originated faith.
JAMES 2:1 MSG

Are you willing to stand firm against society's untrue messages? And are you willing to stand up for your faith? If so, you'll be doing yourself a king-sized favor. And consider this: When you begin to speak up for God, isn't it logical to assume that you'll also begin to know Him in a more meaningful way? Of course you will.

So do yourself and your loved ones a favor: forget the media hype, and pay attention to God. Stand up for Him and be counted, not just in church where it's relatively easy to be a Christian, but also outside the church, where it's significantly harder. You owe it to God . . . and you owe it to yourself.

more stuff to think about

What is courage? It is the ability to be strong in trust, in conviction, in obedience. To be courageous is to step out in faith—to trust and obey, no matter what.

KAY ARTHUR

Consider seriously how quickly people change, and how little trust is to be had in them; and cleave fast unto God, who changeth not.

ST. TERESA OF AVILA

With God, it's never "Plan B" or "second best."
It's always "Plan A." And, if we let Him,
He'll make something beautiful of our lives.

GLORIA GAITHER

The Big Idea

Compare the amount of time you spend watching TV to the time you spend studying God's Word. If you don't like the results of that comparison, it's time to think long and hard about the difference between the media's priorities and God's priorities.

DATING & SEX

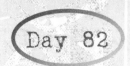

Take the Positive Path

But the path of the just is like the shining sun, that shines ever brighter unto the perfect day. The way of the wicked is like darkness; they do not know what makes them stumble.

Proverbs 4:18-19 NKJV

When Jesus addressed His disciples, He warned that each one must, "take up his cross and follow me." The disciples must have known exactly what the Master meant. In Jesus' day, prisoners were forced to carry their own crosses to the location where they would be put to death. Thus, Christ's message was clear: in order to follow Him, Christ's disciples must deny themselves and, instead, trust Him completely. Nothing has changed since then.

If we are to be dutiful disciples of the One from Galilee, we must trust Him and we must follow Him. Jesus never comes "next." He is always first. He shows us the path of life.

Do you seek to be a worthy disciple of Jesus? Then pick up His cross today and follow in His footsteps. When you do, you can walk with confidence: He will never lead you astray.

2 minutes A DAY

To a world that was spiritually dry and populated with parched lives scorched by sin, [Jesus] was the Living Water who would quench the thirsty soul, saving it from "bondage" and filling it with satisfaction and joy and purpose and meaning.

ANNE GRAHAM LOTZ

If doing a good act in public will excite others to do more good, then "Let your Light shine to all,"
Miss no opportunity to do good.

JOHN WESLEY

Be such a person, and live such a life, that if every person were such as you, and every life a life like yours, this earth would be God's Paradise.

PHILLIPS BROOKS

The Big Idea

Do you believe that you're working, not just for yourself, but also for God. If you said yes, you're right.

DATING & SEX

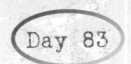

Be Careful How You Direct Your Thoughts

Finally, brothers, whatever is true, whatever is noble, whatever is right, whatever is pure, whatever is lovely, whatever is admirable—if anything is excellent or praiseworthy—think about such things.

PHILIPPIANS 4:8 NIV

How will you direct your thoughts today? Will you obey the words of Philippians 4:8 by dwelling upon those things that are honorable, true, and worthy of praise? Or will you allow your thoughts to be hijacked by the negativity that seems to dominate our troubled world.

Are you fearful, angry, bored, or worried? Are you so preoccupied with the concerns of this day that you fail to thank God for the promise of eternity? Are you confused, bitter, or pessimistic? If so, God wants to have a little talk with you. He wants to remind you of His infinite love and His boundless grace. As you contemplate these things, and as you give thanks for God's blessings, negativity should no longer dominate your day or your life.

2 minutes A DAY

more stuff to think about

Our own possible bad thoughts and deeds are far more dangerous to us than any enemy from the world.

St. Ambrose

We know well enough how to keep outward silence, and to hush our spoken words, but we know little of interior silence. It consists in hushing our idle, restless, wandering imagination, in quieting the promptings of our worldly minds, and in suppressing the crowd of unprofitable thoughts which excite and disturb the soul.

François Fènelon

People who do not develop and practice good thinking often find themselves at the mercy of their circumstances.

John Maxwell

The Big Idea

Good thoughts can lead you to some very good places . . . and bad thoughts can lead elsewhere. So guard your thoughts accordingly.

DATING & SEX

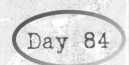

Put Holiness Before Happiness

*Blessed are those who hunger and thirst for righteousness,
for they will be filled.*

MATTHEW 5:6 NIV

Because you are an imperfect human being, you are not "perfectly" happy, and you won't have "perfect" relationships—and that's perfectly okay with God. He is far less concerned with your happiness than He is with your holiness.

God continuously reveals Himself in everyday life, but He does not do so in order to make you contented; He does so in order to lead you to His Son. So don't be overly concerned with your current level of happiness: it will change. Be more concerned with the current state of your relationship with Christ: He does not change. And because your Savior transcends time and space, you can be comforted in the knowledge that in the end, His joy will become your joy . . . for all eternity.

more stuff to think about

You don't have to be like the world to have an impact on the world. You don't have to be like the crowd to change the crowd. You don't have to lower yourself down to their level to lift them up to your level. Holiness doesn't seek to be odd. Holiness seeks to be like God.

MAX LUCADO

Holiness isn't in a style of dress. It's not a matter of rules and regulations. It's a way of life that emanates quietness and rest, joy in family, shared pleasures with friends, the help of a neighbor—and the hope of a Savior.

JONI EARECKSON TADA

The Big Idea

God is holy and wants you to be holy. Christ died to make you holy. Make sure that your response to Christ's sacrifice is worthy of Him.

DATING & SEX

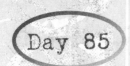
Place a High Value on Yourself and Your Gifts

I remind you to fan into flame the gift of God.

2 TIMOTHY 1:6 NIV

Face it: you've got an array of talents that need to be refined. All people possess special gifts—bestowed from the Father above—and you are no exception. But, your gift is no guarantee of success; it must be cultivated—by you—or it will go unused . . . and God's gift to you will be squandered.

Today, make a promise to yourself that you will earnestly seek to discover the talents that God has given you. Then, nourish those talents and make them grow. Finally, vow to share your gifts with the world for as long as God gives you the power to do so. After all, the best way to say "Thank You" for God's gifts is to use them.

2 minutes A DAY

You are a unique blend of talents, skills, and gifts, which makes you an indispensable member of the body of Christ.

CHARLES STANLEY

Natural abilities are like natural plants;
they need pruning by study.

FRANCIS BACON

You are the only person on earth who can use your ability.

ZIG ZIGLAR

The Big Idea

Today, take time to think about ways you can convert your talents into results.

DATING & SEX

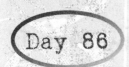

Lasting Relationships Are Built Upon Trust

These are the things you must do: Speak truth to one another; render honest and peaceful judgments in your gates.
ZECHARIAH 8:16 HOLMAN CSB

Lasting relationships are built upon honesty and trust. Without trust, people soon drift apart. But with trust, relationships grow and flourish.

As Christians, we should always try to be trustworthy, encouraging, and loyal. And, we should be thankful for the people who are loyal to us.

Do you want friends you can trust? Then start by being a friend they can trust. And do you want to build relationships that stand the test of time? Then build them on a firm foundation of trust—no shaky foundations, please!

2 minutes A DAY

more stuff to think about

Trust is like "money in the bank" in a marriage.
There must be a reasonable amount of it on deposit to
ensure the security of a marital union.

ED YOUNG

Whatever you do when conflicts arise, be wise. Fight against
jumping to quick conclusions and seeing only your side.
There are always two sides on the streets of conflict.
Look both ways.

CHARLES SWINDOLL

The single most important element in any human relationship
is honesty—with oneself, with God, and with others.

CATHERINE MARSHALL

The Big Idea

Trust is the foundation of meaningful relationships. If you
want your relationship to last, be honest and trustworthy. If
you want a second or third-class relationship, be deceptive,
evasive, and sneaky.

DATING & SEX

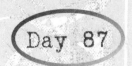

Have a Healthy Fear of God

Since we are receiving a Kingdom that cannot be destroyed, let us be thankful and please God by worshiping him with holy fear and awe.

HEBREWS 12:28 NLT

D o you possess a healthy, fearful respect for God's power? Hopefully so. After all, the lesson from the Book of Proverbs is clear: "The fear of the LORD is the beginning of knowledge, but fools despise wisdom and instruction" (1:7 NKJV). Yet, you live in a world that often ignores the role that God plays in shaping the affairs of mankind. You live in a world where too many people consider it "unfashionable" or "unseemly" to discuss the fear of God. Don't count yourself among their number.

God maintains absolute sovereignty over His creation, and His power is beyond comprehension. As believers, we must cultivate a sincere respect for God's awesome power. The fear of the Lord is, indeed, the beginning of knowledge. So today, as you face the realities of everyday life, remember this: until you acquire a healthy, respectful fear of God's power, your education is incomplete, and so is your faith.

more stuff to think about

When true believers are awed by the greatness of God and by the privilege of becoming His children, then they become sincerely motivated, effective evangelists.

BILL HYBELS

A healthy fear of God will do much to deter us from sin.

CHARLES SWINDOLL

The fear of God is the death of every other fear.

C. H. SPURGEON

The Big Idea

It's the right kind of fear: Your respect for God should make you fearful of disobeying Him . . . very fearful.

DATING & SEX

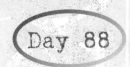
Remember That You Can Always Escape Temptation

The Lord knows how to deliver the godly out of temptations.
2 PETER 2:9 NKJV

If you feel like you're being boxed in by temptations, remember this: you're never completely trapped—there's always an escape hatch. And how, you ask, can you find the way out? Well, you can start by talking to God.

Beth Moore observed, "Because Christ has faced our every temptation without sin, we never face a temptation that has no door of escape." Her words apply to you.

So the next time you face a strong urge to do something wrong, slow yourself down and have a little chat with your Creator. When you talk to Him—sincerely, prayerfully, and as often as necessary—you can overcome any temptation. No exceptions.

more stuff to think about

Do not fight the temptation in detail. Turn from it.
Look ONLY at your Lord. Sing. Read. Work.

AMY CARMICHAEL

Instant intimacy is one of the leading warning signals
of a seduction.

BETH MOORE

Flee temptation without leaving a forwarding address.

BARBARA JOHNSON

The Big Idea

Tempted to do something you know isn't right? Spend just
five minutes praying about it, and then see if you feel the
same level of temptation after you've finished praying.

DATING & SEX

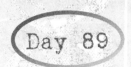

Be Determined to Overcome the World

For whatever is born of God overcomes the world.
And this is the victory that has overcome the world—our faith.

1 JOHN 5:4 NKJV

We live in the world, but we should not worship it— yet at every turn, or so it seems, we are tempted to do otherwise. As Warren Wiersbe correctly observed, "Because the world is deceptive, it is dangerous."

The 21st-century world we live in is a noisy, distracting place, a place that offers countless temptations and dangers. The world seems to cry, "Worship me with your time, your money, your energy, your thoughts, and your life!" But if we are wise, we won't fall prey to that temptation.

C. S. Lewis said, "Aim at heaven and you will get earth thrown in; aim at earth and you will get neither." That's good advice. You're likely to hit what you aim at, so aim high . . . aim at heaven.

more stuff to think about

The world's sewage system threatens to contaminate
the stream of Christian thought.
Is the world shaping your mind, or is Christ?

BILLY GRAHAM

Nothing is more foolish than a security built upon
the world and its promises, for they are all vanity and a lie.

MATTHEW HENRY

A fish would never be happy living on land, because it was
made for water. An eagle could never feel satisfied
if it wasn't allowed to fly. You will never feel completely
satisfied on earth, because you were made for more.

RICK WARREN

The Big Idea

The world's power to distract, detour, and destroy is
formidable. Thankfully, God's power is even greater.

DATING & SEX

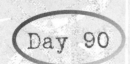

Day 90

Decide How You'll Behave Yourself Before the Date (Not During the Date!)

The prudent see danger and take refuge,
but the simple keep going and suffer from it.
PROVERBS 27:12 NIV

If you continue to date somebody who behaves foolishly or impulsively, then sooner or later, you'll probably find yourself doing impulsive things, too. And that's bad . . . very bad. So here's an ironclad rule for maintaining your self-respect and your sanity: If you find yourself out on a date with an impulsive person who's pressuring you to betray your values, go home and go home fast. Otherwise, before you know it, you'll be in more trouble than you can imagine.

When you feel pressured to do things—or to compromise yourself—in ways that lead you away from God, you're heading straight for major-league problems The best time to decide how you'll behave yourself is before you go out on a date (not during a date!). So don't do the "easy" thing and don't do the impulsive thing. Do the right thing, and do it every time.

2 minutes A DAY

more stuff to think about

Holiness is not inability to sin, but ability not to sin.

G. CAMPBELL MORGAN

There may be no trumpet sound or loud applause
when we make a right decision, just a calm sense of
resolution and peace.

GLORIA GAITHER

Obedience is the outward expression of your love of God.

HENRY BLACKABY

The Big Idea

If you can't seem to put the brakes on impulsive behavior . . .
you're not praying hard enough.

DATING & SEX

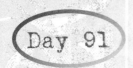

Don't Give in to Pessimism

Give your worries to the Lord, and he will take care of you.
He will never let good people down.
PSALM 55:22 NCV

Pessimism and Christianity don't mix. Why? Because Christians have every reason to be optimistic about life here on earth and life eternal. As C. H. Spurgeon observed, "Our hope in Christ for the future is the mainstream of our joy." But sometimes, we fall prey to worry, frustration, anxiety, or sheer exhaustion, and our hearts become heavy. What's needed is plenty of rest, a large dose of perspective, and God's healing touch, but not necessarily in that order.

Today, make this promise to yourself and keep it: vow to be a hope-filled Christian. Think optimistically about your life, your family, your future, and your friends. Trust your hopes, not your fears. Take time to celebrate God's glorious creation. And then, when you've filled your heart with hope and gladness, share your optimism with your friends and loved ones. They'll be better for it, and so will you. But not necessarily in that order.

2 MINUTES A DAY

A pessimist is someone who believes that when her cup runneth over she'll need a mop.

BARBARA JOHNSON

To lose heart is to lose everything.

JOHN ELDREDGE

Never yield to gloomy anticipation. Place your hope and confidence in God. He has no record of failure.

MRS. CHARLES E. COWMAN

The Big Idea

If you genuinely believe that God is good and that His Son died for your sins, how can you be pessimistic about your future? The answer, of course, is that you can't!

DATING & SEX

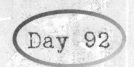

Put Faith Above Feelings

Now the just shall live by faith.
HEBREWS 10:38 NKJV

Hebrews 10:38 teaches that we should live by faith. Yet sometimes, despite our best intentions, negative feelings can rob us of the peace and abundance that would otherwise be ours through Christ. When anger or anxiety separates us from the spiritual blessings that God has in store, we must rethink our priorities and renew our faith. And we must place faith above feelings. Human emotions are highly variable, decidedly unpredictable, and often unreliable. Our emotions are like the weather, only far more fickle. So we must learn to live by faith, not by the ups and downs of our own emotional roller coasters.

Sometime during this day, you will probably be gripped by a strong negative emotion. Distrust it. Reign it in. Test it. And turn it over to God. Your emotions will inevitably change; God will not. So trust Him completely as you watch your feelings slowly evaporate into thin air—which, of course, they will.

more stuff to think about

We are to live by faith, not feelings.
KAY ARTHUR

It gives me a deep, comforting sense that
"things seen are temporal and things unseen are eternal."
HELEN KELLER

Sometimes the very essence of faith is trusting God in
the midst of things He knows good and well we cannot
comprehend.
BETH MOORE

The Big Idea

Do you trust Him completely? If you genuinely trust God, it
means you don't have to understand everything.

DATING & SEX

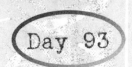

Day 93

When It Comes to Sin, Don't Be Neutral

So put to death the sinful, earthly things lurking within you. Have nothing to do with sexual sin, impurity, lust, and shameful desires. Don't be greedy for the good things of this life, for that is idolatry. God's terrible anger will come upon those who do such things.

COLOSSIANS 3:5-6 NLT

Nineteenth-century clergyman Edwin Hubbel Chapin warned, "Neutral men are the devil's allies." His words were true then, and they're true now. Neutrality in the face of evil is a sin. Yet all too often, we fail to fight evil, not because we are neutral, but because we are shortsighted: we don't fight the devil because we don't recognize his handiwork.

If we are to recognize evil and fight it, we must pay careful attention. We must pay attention to God's Word, and we must pay attention to the realities of everyday life. When we observe life objectively, and when we do so with eyes and hearts that are attuned to God's Holy Word, we can no longer be neutral believers. And when we are no longer neutral, God rejoices while the devil despairs.

more stuff to think about

The greatest enemy of holiness is not passion; it is apathy.

JOHN ELDREDGE

Jesus calls you to be a non-conformist.
Live to be separated from the evils of the world.
Live to be different.

BILLY GRAHAM

The committed man of God is against sin,
and all the powers of evil are against him.
In such a warfare there is no intermission at all.
The devil never takes even a five-minute vacation.

ALAN REDPATH

The Big Idea

Evil does exist, and you will confront it. Prepare yourself by forming a genuine, life-changing relationship with God and His only begotten Son.

DATING & SEX

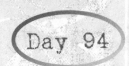

Keep Your Heart Pure

Everything is pure to those whose hearts are pure.
But nothing is pure to those who are corrupt and unbelieving,
because their minds and consciences are defiled.

TITUS 1:15 NLT

You are near and dear to God. He loves you more than you can imagine, and He wants the very best for you. And one more thing: God wants you to guard your heart.

Every day, you are faced with choices . . . lots of them. You can do the right thing, or not. You can tell the truth, or not. You can be kind and generous and obedient. Or not.

Today, the world will offer you countless opportunities to let down your guard and, by doing so, let the devil do his worst. Be watchful and obedient. Guard your heart by giving it to your Heavenly Father; it is safe with Him.

more stuff to think about

Religious activity can never substitute for a heart
that is pure before Him.
HENRY BLACKABY

Those whose hearts are pure are the temples
of the Holy Spirit.
LUCI SWINDOLL

Spiritual truth is discernable only to a pure heart,
not to a keen intellect. It is not a question of
profundity of intellect, but of purity of heart.
OSWALD CHAMBERS

The Big Idea

Accept God's love . . . and love God in return. God loves
you for who you are, not because of the things you've done.
So open your heart to God's love . . . when you do, you'll
feel better about everything, including yourself.

DATING & SEX

Don't Underestimate the Importance of Your Friends

As iron sharpens iron, a friend sharpens a friend.
PROVERBS 27:17 NLT

Are your closest friends the kind of people who encourage you to behave yourself? And are you a better person because of those relationships? If so, you've chosen your friends wisely.

But if your friends encourage you to do things that you know to be wrong, perhaps it's time to think long and hard about making some new friends.

Whether you realize it or not, you're probably going to behave like your friends behave. So pick out friends who make you want to become a better person. When you do, you'll be saving yourself from a lot of trouble . . . make that a whole lot of trouble.

2 minutes a day

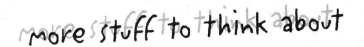

more stuff to think about

A true friend is the gift of God.

ROBERT SOUTH

Yes, the Spirit was sent to be our Counselor.
Yes, Jesus speaks to us personally.
But often he works through another human being.

JOHN ELDREDGE

A friend is one who makes me do my best.

OSWALD CHAMBERS

The Big Idea

Your friends will have a major impact on your self-image.
That's an important reason (but not the only reason) to select
your friends carefully.

DATING & SEX

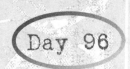

Day 96

Remember That God Is Watching

*So I strive always to keep my conscience clear
before God and man.*

ACTS 24:16 NIV

You can keep some secrets from other people, but you can't keep any secrets from God. God knows what you think and what you do. And, if you want to please Him, you must start with good intentions and a pure heart.

If your heart tells you not to do something, don't do it! If your conscience tells you that something is wrong, stop! If you feel ashamed by something you've done, don't do it ever again! And if your spirit is being crushed by a relationship you're in, escape!

And while you're at it, don't do anything that you wouldn't do if God were standing right behind you, looking over your shoulder . . . because He is.

2 minutes a day

more stuff to think about

God cannot lead the individual who is not willing to give
Him a blank check with his life.

CATHERINE MARSHALL

Anyone can count the seeds in an apple,
but only God can count the number of apples in a seed.

ROBERT SCHULLER

God grades on the cross, not the curve.

ANONYMOUS

The Big Idea

Of course we know that God watches over us, but we must
also make certain that our friends know that we know. And,
we must behave in ways that let our friends know that we
know that He knows. Whew!

DATING & SEX

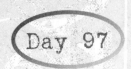

Get Wisdom, Be Happy

To acquire wisdom is to love oneself;
people who cherish understanding will prosper.
PROVERBS 19:8 NLT

The world has its own brand of wisdom, a brand of wisdom that is often wrong and sometimes dangerous. God, on the other hand, has a different brand of wisdom, a wisdom that will never lead you astray. Where will you place your trust today? Will you trust in the wisdom of fallible people, or will you place your faith in God's perfect wisdom? The answer to this question will determine the direction of your day and the quality of your relationships.

Are you tired? Discouraged? Fearful? Be comforted and trust God. Are you worried or anxious? Be confident in God's power. Are you confused? Listen to the quiet voice of your Heavenly Father—He is not a God of confusion. Talk with Him; listen to Him; trust Him. His wisdom, unlike the "wisdom" of the world, will never let you down.

2 minutes A DAY

more stuff to think about

The process of living seems to consist in coming to realize truths so ancient and simple that, if stated, they sound like barren platitudes. They cannot sound otherwise to those who have not had the relevant experience: that is why there is no real teaching of such truths possible and every generation starts from scratch.

C. S. LEWIS

The Spirit of God is direct, authoritative, the foundation of wisdom, life, and holiness.

ST. JOHN OF DAMASCUS

This is my song through endless ages: Jesus led me all the way.

FANNY CROSBY

The Big Idea

Don't be satisfied with the acquisition of knowledge . . . strive to acquire wisdom. As Beth Moore correctly observed, "A big difference exists between a head full of knowledge and the words of God literally abiding in us."

DATING & SEX

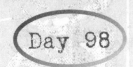

Have a Chat with God Every Morning

*Morning by morning he wakens me and opens
my understanding to his will.
The Sovereign LORD has spoken to me, and I have listened.*
ISAIAH 50:4-5 NLT

D o you want to know God better? And do you want to let Him help you build strong, healthy relationships? Then schedule a meeting with Him every day.

Daily life is a tapestry of habits, and no habit is more important to your spiritual health than the discipline of daily prayer and devotion to the Creator. When you begin each day with your head bowed and your heart lifted, you are reminded of God's love and God's laws.

When you do engage in a regular regimen of worship and praise, God will reward you for your wisdom and your obedience.

more stuff to think about

A person with no devotional life generally struggles
with faith and obedience.

CHARLES STANLEY

The moment you wake up each morning, all your wishes and
hopes for the day rush at you like wild animals. And the first
job each morning consists in shoving it all back; in listening
to that other voice, taking that other point of view, letting that
other, larger, stronger, quieter life come flowing in.

C. S. LEWIS

Devotional books have an important ministry,
but they are never substitutes for your Bible.

WARREN WIERSBE

The Big Idea

The right way to start the day? Begin it with a few minutes of
quiet time to organize your thoughts. During this time, read
at least one uplifting Bible passage and thus begin your day
on a positive, productive note.

DATING & SEX

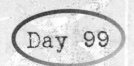

Day 99

When It Comes to Your Relationships, Your Choices Have Major Consequences

*Wisdom is pleasing to you. If you find it,
you have hope for the future.*
PROVERBS 24:14 NCV

Your life is an adventure in decision-making . . . and the same thing can be said of your relationships. If you want to build strong, Christ-centered relationships, you must make wise decisions, and you must make them consistently.

Each day, all of us make countless decisions that hopefully bring us closer to God. When we obey God's commandments, we share in His abundance and His peace. But, when we turn our backs upon God by disobeying Him, we invite Old Man Trouble to stop by for an extended visit.

Do you want to be successful in life and in love? If so, here's a good place to start: Obey God. When you're faced with a difficult choice or a powerful temptation, pray about it. Invite God into your heart and live according to His commandments. When you do, you will be blessed today and tomorrow and forever.

The Reference Point for the Christian is the Bible.
All values, judgments, and attitudes must be gauged in
relationship to this Reference Point.

RUTH BELL GRAHAM

Never make a decision without stopping to consider
the matter in the presence of God.

JOSEMARIA ESCRIVA

God always gives His best to those who leave
the choice with Him.

JIM ELLIOT

The Big Idea

First you'll make choices . . . and before you know it, your
choices will make you. So choose carefully.

DATING & SEX

Walk With the Man from Galilee

Then he told them what they could expect for themselves:
"Anyone who intends to come with me has to let me lead."

LUKE 9:23 MSG

Here's one last tip for your dating life: behave yourself like a Christian every day of the week, not just on Sundays. In other words, make Jesus a priority in every aspect of your life, including your dating life.

Jesus made an extreme sacrifice for you. Are you willing to make changes in your life for Him? Can you honestly say that you're passionate about your faith and that you're really following Jesus? Hopefully so. But if you're preoccupied with other things—or if you're strictly a one-day-a-week Christian—then you're in need of a big time spiritual makeover.

Jesus doesn't want you to be a run-of-the-mill, follow-the-crowd kind of believer. Jesus wants you to be a "new creation" through Him. And that's exactly what you should want for yourself, too.

So remember this: you're the recipient of Christ's love. Accept it enthusiastically and demonstrate your love with words and actions. Jesus deserves your heart—give it to Him today, tomorrow, and forever, Amen.

more stuff to think about

When we truly walk with God throughout our day,
life slowly starts to fall into place.

BILL HYBELS

As we trust God to give us wisdom for today's decisions,
He will lead us a step at a time into what
He wants us to be doing in the future.

THEODORE EPP

Walk in the daylight of God's will because
then you will be safe; you will not stumble.

ANNE GRAHAM LOTZ

The Big Idea

If you want to follow in Christ's footsteps . . . welcome Him
into your heart, obey His commandments, and share His
never-ending love.

DATING & SEX